CHATS WITH CONVERTS

COMPLETE EXPLANATION AND PROOF OF CATHOLIC BELIEF

BY

REV. M. D. FORREST, M.S.C.

with Preface by

BISHOP FULTON J. SHEEN, Ph.D., D.D., L.L.D.

31st Printing

TAN BOOKS AND PUBLISHERS, INC.
Rockford, Illinois 61105

Dedication

To St. Therese of the Child Jesus, the Little Flower, styled by Pope Pius XI as "my guiding star" and "the child beloved of the world," whose virginal heart ever glowed with living zeal for souls, who expressed the ardent wish to "spend her heaven in doing good on earth," these *Chats with Prospective Converts* are humbly, gratefully, and lovingly dedicated.

IMPRIMATUR:

N. T. Gilroy
Archbishop of Sydney

ISBN: 0-89555-069-5

Library of Congress Catalog Card Number: 78-56979

Printed and bound in the United States of America

TAN BOOKS AND PUBLISHERS, INC.
P.O. Box 424
Rockford, Illinois 61105

1978

AUTHOR'S FOREWORD

These "Chats with Converts" have already appeared as a series of articles in the "New Zealand Tablet," and the Sydney "Catholic Weekly," and are now published in book form with permission of the management of those excellent journals.

My purpose in publishing this book is to furnish instructors with a Manual for Converts; but I hope that the work will be of some help also to Study Clubs and to the senior pupils of our schools in their study of Apologetics.

In writing these articles, I had in mind a course of instructions extending over a period of about six months, with one lesson a week; or of three months, with two talks a week. Though I am of opinion that this should be the normal course of preparation for a convert, I am aware that at times converts have to be instructed and received within a shorter period. In the latter case the instructor should either choose what he considers the more important subjects or condense and summarize the matter of each chapter.

I wish to place on record my grateful appreciation of the many kind messages of encouragement and approval received from readers, clerical and lay, while the series was appearing in the two Catholic papers mentioned, and to express my sincerest gratitude to His Grace, the Archbishop of Sydney, for graciously and gracefully writing the Foreword.

Through the great courtesy, unflagging zeal, and efficient management of the nationally known Rev. Charles M. Carty, I now have the pleasure of presenting this new edition to the American public.

M. D. FORREST, M. S. C.,
Sacred Heart Monastery,
Croydon, Victoria, Australia.

FOREWORD

As you would that men should do to you,
do you also to them in like manner.

THUS spoke the Divine Teacher. The lesson was for men of the twentieth century as for those of the first: for you, and me, as for the Jews of old.

If you were bewildered and vainly sought for the path that would lead to your destination, you would be grateful for the guidance of anyone who, knowing the way, shared his knowledge of it with you.

The articles written in this book by Father M. D. Forrest, M.S.C., will assist every Catholic layman to be such a guide, warning of danger and indicating safety.

Just as eternity is of greater importance than time, the soul of greater importance than the body, so is it more important to warn men of dangers to salvation than of dangers to life, more charitable to indicate the path to Heaven than to any destination here below.

Nearly all have friends and acquaintances who are journeying along the road of life without ever thinking seriously of the eternity that awaits them.

The safe road through life: the road to Heaven along which every earthly pilgrim (and each of us is only that) may travel if he so desires, was indicated by Our Lord and Savior, Jesus Christ. It is indicated today by the Church which Christ Himself established for that purpose.

To tell men who do not know it of the existence of that safe and sure path to Heaven, to show them how to reach and traverse it, is the apostolate, the honorable apostolate, every Catholic layman may exercise.

These Chats of Father Forrest, himself an apostolic Priest remarkable for his learning and zeal, will assist laymen to understand more clearly how precious is the treasure of which they are custodians; will assist and encourage them to share with others God's greatest gift to man, the True Faith.

✠ N. T. GILROY,
Archbishop of Sydney.

IMPRIMATUR:
✠ N. T. GILROY,
Archiepiscopus Sydneyensis.

The Preface by Bishop Fulton J. Sheen, D.D., to the Third Volume of Radio Replies brought so many favorable letters from converts to our office that we are reprinting the same message because of its merit and popularity as a Preface to this companion book to the three volumes of Radio Replies by Fathers Rumble and Carty.

PREFACE

ONCE there were lost islands, but most of them have been found; once there were lost causes, but many of them have been retrieved; but there is one lost art that has not been definitely recovered, and without which no civilization can long survive, and that is the art of controversy. The hardest thing to find in the world today is an argument. Because so few are thinking, naturally there are found but few to argue. Prejudice there is in abundance and sentiment too, for these things are born of enthusiasms without the pain of labor. Thinking, on the contrary, is a difficult task; it is the hardest work a man can do—that is perhaps why so few indulge in it. Thought-saving devices have been invented that rival labor-saving devices in their ingenuity. Fine-sounding phrases like "Life is bigger than logic," or "Progress is the spirit of the age," go rattling by us like express trains, carrying the burden of those who are too lazy to think for themselves.

Not even philosophers argue today; they only explain away. A book full of bad logic, advocating all manner of moral laxity, is not refuted by critics; it is merely called "bold, honest, and fearless." Even those periodicals which pride themselves upon their open-mindedness on all questions are far from practicing the lost art of controversy. Their pages contain no controversies, but only presentations of points of view; these never rise to the level of abstract thought in which argument clashes with argument like steel with steel, but rather they content themselves with the personal reflections of one who has lost his faith, writing against the sanctity of marriage, and of another who has kept his faith, writing in favor of it. Both sides are shooting off firecrackers, making all the noise of an intellectual warfare and creating the illusion of conflict, but it is only a sham battle in which there are no casualties; there are plenty of explosions, but never an exploded argument.

The causes underlying this decline in the art of controversy are twofold: religious and philosophical. Modern religion has enunciated one great and fundamental dogma that is at the basis of all the other dogmas, and that is, that religion must be freed from dogmas. Creeds and confessions of faith are no longer the fashion; religious leaders have agreed not to disagree and those beliefs for which some of our ancestors would have died they have melted into a spineless Humanism. Like other Pilates they have turned their backs on the uniqueness of truth and have opened their arms wide to all the moods and fancies the hour might dictate. The passing of creeds and dogmas means the passing of controversies. Creeds and dogmas are social; prejudices are private. Believers bump into one another at a thousand different angles, but bigots keep out of one another's way, because prejudice is anti-social. I can imagine an old-fashioned Calvinist who holds that the word "damn" has a tremendous dogmatic significance, coming to intellectual blows with an old-fashioned Methodist who holds that it is only a curse word; but I cannot imagine a controversy if both decide to damn damnation, like our Modernists who no longer believe in Hell.

The second cause, which is philosophical, bases itself on that peculiar American philosophy called "Pragmatism," the aim of which is to prove that all proofs are useless. Hegel, of Germany, rationalized error; James, of America, derationalized truth. As a result, there has sprung up a disturbing indifference to truth, and a tendency to regard the useful as the true, and the impractical as the false. The man who can make up his mind when proofs are presented to him is looked upon as a bigot, and the man who ignores proofs and the search for truth is looked upon as broad-minded and tolerant.

Another evidence of this same disrespect for rational foundations is the general readiness of the modern mind to accept a statement because of the literary way in which it is couched, or because of the popularity of the one who says it, rather than for the reasons behind the statement. In this sense, it is unfortunate that some men who think poorly can write so well. Bergson has written a philosophy grounded on the assumption that the greater comes from the less, but he has so camouflaged that intellectual monstrosity with mellifluous French that he has been credited with being a great and original thinker. To some minds, of course, the startling will always appear to be the profound. It is easier to get the attention of the press when one says, as Ibsen did, that "two and two make five," than to be orthodox and say that two and two make four.

The Catholic Church perhaps more than the other forms of Christianity notices the decline in the art of controversy. Never before, perhaps, in the whole history of Christianity has she been so intellectually impoverished for want of good, sound intellectual opposition as she is at the present time. Today there are no foe-men worthy of her steel. And if the Church today is not producing great chunks of thought, or what might be called "'thinkage," it is because she has not been challenged to do so. The best in everything comes from the throwing down of a gauntlet—even the best in thought.

The Church loves controversy, and loves it for two reasons: because intellectual conflict is informing, and because she is madly in love with rationalism. The great structure of the Catholic Church has been built up through controversy. It was the attacks of the Docetists and the Monophysites in the early centuries of the Church that made her clear on the doctrine concerning the nature of Christ; it was the controversy with the Reformers that clarified her teaching on justification. And if today there are not nearly so many dogmas defined as in the early ages of the Church, it is because there is less controversy—and less thinking. One must think to be a heretic, even though it be wrong thinking.

Even though one did not accept the infallible authority of the Church, he would still have to admit that the Church in the course of centuries has had her finger on the pulse of the world, ever defining those dogmas which needed definition at the moment. In the light of this fact, it would be interesting to inquire if our boasted theory of intellectual progress is true. What was the Christian world thinking about in the early centuries? What doctrines had to be clarified when controversy was keen? In the early centuries, controversy centered on such lofty and delicate problems as the Trinity, the Incarnation, the union of Natures in the person of the Son of God. What was the last doctrine to be defined in 1870? It was the capability of man to use his brain and come to a knowledge of God. Now, if the world is progressing intellectually, should not the existence of God have been defined in the first century, and the nature of the Trinity have been defined in the nineteenth? In the order of mathematics this is like defining the complexities of logarithms in the year 42, and the simplification of the addition table in the year 1942. The fact is that there is now less intellectual opposition to the Church and more prejudice, which, being interpreted, means less thinking, even less bad thinking.

Not only does the Church love controversy because it helps her sharpen her wits; she loves it also for its own sake. The Church is accused of being the enemy of reason; as a matter of fact, she is the only one who believes in it. Using her reason in the Council of the Vatican, she officially went on record in favor of Rationalism, and declared, against the mock humility of the Agnostics and the sentimental faith of the Fideists, that human reason by its own power can know something besides the contents of test tubes and retorts, and that working on mere sensible phenomena it can soar even to the "hid battlements of eternity," there to discover the Timeless beyond time and the Spaceless beyond space which is God, the Alpha and Omega of all things.

The Church asks her children to think hard and think clean. Then she asks them to do two things with their thoughts: First, she asks them to externalize them in the concrete world of economics, government, commerce, and education, and by this externalization of beautiful, clean thoughts to produce a beautiful and clean civilization. The quality of any civilization depends upon the nature of the thoughts its great minds bequeath to it. If the thoughts that are externalized in the press, in the senate chamber, on the public platform, are base, civilization itself will take on their base character with the same readiness with which a chameleon takes on the color of the object upon which it is placed. But if the thoughts that are vocalized and articulated are high and lofty, civilization will be filled, like a crucible, with the gold of the things worth while.

The Church asks her children not only to externalize their thoughts and thus produce culture, but also to internalize their thoughts and thus produce spirituality. The constant giving would be dissipation unless new energy was supplied from within. In fact, before a thought can be bequeathed to the outside, it must have been born on the inside. But no thought is born without silence and contemplation. It is in the stillness and quiet of one's own intellectual pastures, wherein man meditates on the purpose of life and its goal, that real and true character is developed. A character is made by the kind of thoughts a man thinks when alone, and a civilization is made by the kind of thoughts a man speaks to his neighbor.

On the other hand, the Church discourages bad thinking, for a bad thought set loose is more dangerous than a wild man. Thinkers live; toilers die in a day. When society finds it is too late to electrocute a thought, it electrocutes the man. There was once a time when Christian society burned the thought in order to save society, and after all, something can be said in favor of this practice. To kill one bad thought may mean the salvation of ten thousand thinkers. The Roman emperors were alive to this fact; they killed the Christians not because they wanted their hearts, but because they wanted their heads, or better, their brains—brains that were thinking out the death of Paganism.

It is to this task of thinking out the death of New Paganism that these chapters are published.

BISHOP FULTON J. SHEEN, Ph.D., D.D., L.L.D.

CONTENTS

CONTENTS—Continued

CHAPTER I.

THE EXISTENCE OF GOD

IN our first heart to heart chat, my dear friend, I am going to speak quite simply to you about God, or, in other words, I am going to comment on the first question and answer in our children's Catechism. The question asked is: Who made the world? And the simple answer given is: God.

Now, I do not imply that you need my insistence on this truth, for practically everyone who has come for a chat on religion is already persuaded of it. Indeed, an atheist is as foolish as a boy who would deny that he had a father or mother because he never saw them. And the Scriptures, about which I shall speak later on during the course of our chats, state that only a fool says there is no God. Still, since I intend explaining the whole Catholic religion to you, it will be well to begin with the foundation, even though you already accept it.

Now, our reason clearly shows us that there is a God—a Supreme Being, a Sovereign Lord, a first Cause, an Intelligent, Eternal Power. The normal, rational man perceives, without any difficult process of reasoning, that there is a God, one God, who is endowed with wonderful knowledge, wisdom, and power. I shall give you some of the proofs of God's existence, without burdening you with any difficult scientific terms or abstruse principles of philosophy. Of course, if at any time you wish to delve more deeply into this matter, I

1

shall gladly do so with you or recommend to you pamphlets and books which treat of this truth in a more learned way.

ORDER AND DESIGN.

The order and design everywhere discernible is a clear proof of God's existence. You are familiar with the terms **order, design, purpose,** for they are frequently used in our daily conversation. Order really means unity in variety, or harmony amidst a number of elements. We say that there is order in the arrangement of the various parts of a building, in the combination of the various parts of a motor-car, in the different parts of a clock. By order we mean that a number of things are so arranged as to give a single effect or result. The arrangement of the parts of a house—the bricks or boards, the cement or mortar or nails, the floor, the windows, the ceiling, the roof, etc.— so as to produce the single effect known as a dwelling, is a simple example of order. The word **design** or **purpose** is sometimes used instead of **order** when the first simple proof of God's existence is given. But order is really the result or effect of design or purpose; design means planning order or devising a suitable arrangement. There can be no true order without design or purpose, as there can be no effective designing without order.

The argument drawn from order and design might be stated thus: The evident order that exists throughout our earth and, indeed, throughout the visible universe, the undoubted prevalence of universal law, and the clear adaptation of means to ends convince any reasonable, normal individual that all things that we see have been arranged by a Being external to the world and that this Being must have the greatest knowledge, wisdom, and power.

Look at the printed page before you. Is it conceivable that, by throwing up thousands of letters and letting them fall at random, such an orderly arrangement, consisting of words and sentences, all expressing consecutive thought, could be produced? No one in his right mind would say yes. And yet the order of a typed page is as nothing compared with the order of the vast universe or the order discernible in even a small organic faculty such as the eye or the ear. If the typed or printed page clearly tells of an intelligent and skilful agent behind it, what of the great world and each of the marvellous things we see in it?

Just consider our own earth. It rotates on its axis once every twenty-four hours before the great sun and thus gives us successive day and night. It revolves round the sun once every three hundred and sixty-five days while its axis is constantly inclined to the plane of its orbit at an angle of 66½ degrees, and thus are caused the successive seasons. Here we have evident expression of wondrous intelligence and skill. Then consider our solar system and the whole stellar system, and the marvellous order so clearly telling of the Great Designer overwhelms us.

But I must not lead you too far into the realms of astronomy. I may, however, narrate a simple incident, told by a non-Catholic writer: One fine night on deck, amid a clatter of materialism, Bonaparte pointed to the stars and said: "You may talk as long as you please, gentlemen, but who made all that?"

Joseph Addison has written a beautiful poem which I may appropriately quote for you in this chat:

The spacious firmament on high,
With all the blue ethereal sky,
And spangled heavens, a shining frame,
Their great Original proclaim.
Th' unwearied sun from day to day
Does his Creator's power display;
And publishes, to every land,
The work of an almighty hand.

Soon as the evening shades prevail,
The moon takes up the wondrous tale;
And nightly, to the listening earth
Repeats the story of her birth;
Whilst all the stars that round her burn,
And all the planets in their turn,
Confirm the tidings as they roll,
And spread the truth from pole to pole.

What, though, in solemn silence, all
Move round the dark terrestrial ball;
What though nor real voice nor sound
Amidst their radiant orbs be found;
In reason's ear they all rejoice,
And utter forth a glorious voice,
For ever singing as they shine:
The Hand that made us is Divine.

We might descend to smaller things and see how design is stamped on every inorganic (non-living) and organic (living) being in this world, but it will suffice to draw your attention to a few examples. Take the human eye, for instance. It is like a living camera, and is as manifestly designed for the purpose of seeing as the camera is for the purpose of photographing. The ear, too, displays a wondrous mechanism; in fact, some consider it more wonderful than the eye. Even the scoffer, Voltaire, wrote: "To affirm that the eye is not made to see, nor the ear to hear, nor the stomach to digest food, would be the most monstrous absurdity and the most revolting stupidity that ever beset a human mind. Sceptical as I am, I declare such to be evident madness." He who made the eye to see and the ear to hear and the lungs to breathe must, indeed, be a Designer of surpassing knowledge and consummate skill, endowed with knowledge and power and skill immeasurably beyond the perfections of any human genius.

CAUSE AND EFFECT.

Another proof of God's existence is known as the argument from **causality**. It may be briefly stated thus: All around us we see effects proceeding from causes and causes producing effects. An **effect** is something brought into existence by something else, e.g., steam is produced by heat and water. A **cause** is that which brings into existence or produces something else, i.e., that which produces an effect. Thus a bullet discharged from a rifle is the cause of the mortal wound inflicted on a rabbit. Now, our experience tells us that every cause that comes under our observation is itself produced by another cause; that it is the effect of another cause. In a word, every cause that comes within the range of our experience is a **subordinate** or **dependent cause.** But our reason tells us that the whole series of causes, no matter how far back we may go, must have a **First Cause,** a cause that is not also an effect, an uncaused cause; else we should have an infinite number of causes (which is a contradiction), and, besides, this infinite number of finite causes would still need its own; for, if each member of the series is caused, the whole series likewise is caused. Thus, in sheer logic or commonsense, we **must** get outside all caused causes or finite causes and arrive at an uncaused or First Cause, the Being that is self-existent and eternal, whom we call God.

I have but summarized this proof for you. A book might be written on it, but I must keep to our simple chats.

OTHER PROOFS

There are other proofs of God's existence, but what I have said will be quite sufficient for one chat. I could outline the argument from conscience, from the laws of nature, from motion, from dependent (or contingent) beings, from the dissipation or degradation of energy (a scientific proof), and the persuasion of mankind. But I am not giving you a treatise on God's existence.

Remember, too, my dear friend, that there is such a thing as blinding one's mind or dulling one's moral sense by pride or impurity or avarice, and that God may not be intellectually or spiritually perceived by a soul afflicted by or addicted to one of these vices. "Blessed are the clean of heart, for they shall see God. . . . God resists the proud and gives grace to the humble." The proofs of God's existence are conclusive, though not coercive; sufficient, though not resistless; convincing, though not compelling. They are clear to all whose minds are normal and whose wills and hearts are honest and upright.

DIMNESS OF HUMAN REASON

Although human reason can prove that there is a God and can grasp the fundamental truths or principles of religion and morality, still the natural light of our mind is but dim. But God, in His goodness, has not left us poor mortals groping in the dim twilight of unaided reason, as I shall explain in our next chat.

CHAPTER II.

REVELATION AND FAITH

THE purpose of the present chat, my dear inquirer, is to prepare you for the acceptance of God's revelation by an act of faith. I shall explain the words **revelation** and **faith** presently. First of all, it will be better to say a few words about **knowledge**, for faith is one kind of knowledge.

THREE KINDS OF KNOWLEDGE

There are three kinds of knowledge, which we may term **evidence, science,** and **faith.**

A truth or fact is evident (or, as some would prefer to say, self-evident) when it can be seen, as it were, in its own light; that is, when it needs no other fact or truth to make it known to us; when it is seen by itself; when it so strikes the senses or the mind that it needs no proof whatever, and cannot be doubted by any normal being. I see a piece of bread on my plate—its existence or presence is evident. I am absolutely conscious that I exist—my own existence is evident.

There are other truths which, though not evident, are clearly deduced or inferred or proved from evident truths. Those who have studied geometry know that in this subject one proceeds from what is evident to what must be proved. Thus we proceed by a process of demonstration to the truth that the three angles of every triangle are equal to two right angles. The latter truth may be called science, or, better, the knowledge of it may be called science. If you wish, you may call the first kind of knowledge (of the presence of the piece of bread, of my existence) self-evidence or immediate evidence, and the second kind of knowledge (that the three angles of a triangle equal two right angles) mediate evidence. If you are not interested in geometry, and want a simpler example, consider book-keeping. It is evident (self-evident) to you that on the first line you have $5.43, that you have $12.24 on the second line, $7.19 on the third line, $16.85 on the fourth line, $74.53 on the fifth line, and $39.44 on the sixth line. To know this you need just look at each line. But the total of all those sums is not evident to you; you must add up those sums to get the total; you must "work out" the answer. But, if you are any good at arithmetic, you will not need any outside help; you will be able to get the answer by your own addition. Your knowledge, however, of the result will be only mediate evidence (or science). I am not here using the term **science** as that branch of study known as physical science.

Besides evidence (self-evidence) and science (mediate evidence), there is another kind of knowledge which is admitted and acted on by all reasonable persons. It is called faith. I am not for the moment speaking of religious faith. I am speaking of ordinary human faith which is exercised even by atheists and agnostics.

We often assent to a truth not because it is immediately or mediately evident (as I have explained), but because it is **revealed** (made known) to us by a **reliable witness** or **authority.**

8

EXPLANATION OF HUMAN FAITH

The reliability of a witness requires two elements, knowledge and veracity. We do not accept a statement made by one whom we know to be quite ignorant of the matter he mentions, or by one whom we know to be lying. Before we can reasonably assent to a truth that is not evident (immediately or mediately) to us, we must be satisfied that the person who reveals or makes known such a truth or fact has true knowledge of what he tells us and that he is speaking truthfully; that is, we must be sure that such a witness is not deceived himself and is not deceiving us. When these two conditions are fulfilled, a witness is said to be **reliable**, and, if we are reasonable, we shall accept the statement made by such a witness. This means, in other words, that every reasonable person must assent to, or accept, a revelation or revealed truth or fact that is proposed for our acceptance by a reliable witness.

Let us consider some simple examples of human faith. You are sick, and a friend sends for a doctor. Your acceptance of the doctor is an act of faith, unless you personally witnessed him follow his medical studies and receive his diploma. The doctor prescribes for you, and you send a messenger with the prescription to the pharmacist. Here you elicit at least two new acts of faith—one in the messenger, the other in the pharmacist. Only by faith you admit that the latter is a true pharmacist (unless, again, you witnessed him qualify), and by faith you accept and take his medicine as corresponding to the doctor's prescription.

Murder has been committed, and a certain man happens to be arrested and brought to trial. The jury is sworn in, and the witnesses give their evidence. It may be that not one of the jurymen knows the prisoner, or has any personal evidence of his guilt. Yet, if it is clear from the trial that the witnesses have evidence that the accused committed the murder and that they are truthful—in a word, that they are reliable witnesses—the jury brings in a verdict of guilty, and the judge pronounces sentence of death. Thus the murderer's execution is the result of an act of faith made by the jury and judge on the testimony of reliable witnesses. Their state of mind might be analyzed thus: "We do not know this man, nor have we any personal evidence that he committed the murder in question. But we believe that he did so, because reliable witnesses (i.e., persons who were neither deceived as to what they stated, nor deceiving us) have revealed or made known or declared that this man committed the murder."

Scientists predict an eclipse of the sun. On the day and hour specified crowds of people, who could not personally calculate an eclipse, gather confidently to witness the event. These people are making a simple act of faith, believing on testimony of reliable men that the eclipse will occur according to schedule. Only when the event actually occurs have they evidence of the eclipse.

Why, our very family life is founded on faith. Only by an act of faith can we accept this man and this woman as our father and mother; only by an act of faith do we accept these girls and these boys as our sisters and brothers.

DIVINE REVELATION AND FAITH

Now, if we accept the testimony of reliable human beings, as we all do in our daily life, surely we should, with far greater reason, assent to truths revealed to us by God. Our reason shows that there is a Supreme Being, the Lord of the universe, the infinite, the eternal One. Our reason clearly tells us that He is infinite Truth—that he must know all things and that He cannot utter an untruth or deceive us. Our reason likewise shows that He may, if He choose, make known to us many truths of which we are ignorant, and that, if He speak, He can make it certain, by divine signs, such as miracles and prophecies, that it is He who is teaching us, even though He employ a human agency.

Before Christ came God gave a revelation to one people whom He chose from amongst the various races. This people was not the most intelligent or most advanced in culture, as we understand it. But God gives His graces freely. The people He specially chose for the Old Testament or Covenant was the Jewish people. But we need not go into that matter at present. I just want to emphasize the fact that God did give a revelation, that He did reveal a religion, before Christ, though such revelation was far less perfect or complete than the Christian revelation.

God raised up holy men, Moses and the Prophets, through whom He made known His truth and His law to the Jewish people. He made it clear that the messengers or teachers He employed—Moses and the Prophets—were sent by Him or used by Him to give His revelation to men. How did He make it clear that they were speaking in His name, or that He was speaking through them? He did so by endowing these men with extraordinary holiness and by granting them the gift of prophecy—of foretelling future free events known only to Him—or giving them the power to perform miracles—works that only God can perform. The gift of prophecy and the power to work miracles were like a divine seal stamped on the message these men delivered to God's chosen people.

But the great revelation of God to man—the fulness of Divine Revelation—has come through Jesus Christ, who is not merely a Divine Messenger or Ambassador, but the very Son of God made man, that is, God Incarnate.

CHAPTER III.

THE NEW TESTAMENT AS AN HISTORICAL DOCUMENT

IN this chat, my dear friend, I am going to introduce you to the New Testament (or the New Testament to you). Here is a copy of this wonderful work; I shall give it to you at the end of this talk. Read it carefully.

The New Testament consists of four Gospels (written records of the life of Christ), the Acts of the Apostles (a written record of the first sixty years of Christianity), twenty-one Epistles (letters written by Apostles to their converts), and the Apocalypse or Book of Revelations (the written account of a prophetic vision granted to one of the Apostles in his old age).

I have no intention of giving you a lesson in Scripture. The Catholic Church teaches that each of the written records I have just now mentioned is inspired by God—that, although these works were written by men, the real author is God, who simply made use of human beings as secondary agents. All Protestants, too, or practically all (until recent times), have been strenuous defenders of the inspiration of the Bible—of both the Old and the New Testaments. But there will be time enough later on to talk of inspiration. We must proceed gradually and logically —step by step—in these chats. And at present I am going to consider the books of the New Testament merely as **genuine, truthful, intact, historical records.** Once we have established the reliability of these books, especially of the Gospels, I shall proceed to show how they clearly prove the Divinity of Christ and the truth of His Church.

SPURIOUS AND AUTHENTIC DOCUMENTS

As a witness must be reliable before we can reasonably accept his statement, and as we must assent to his statement if he be reliable, so a document must be reliable before we can reasonably accept what it records, and we must accept what it records if it be reliable. I have already explained what is meant by the reliability of a witness. But what is meant by the reliability of an historical document? What conditions must be fulfilled before its reliability is established?

The simplest way, perhaps, to illustrate this is to consider, first, what is meant by an unreliable document. A document that professes to be reliable or trustworthy may be discredited for one (or more) of three reasons: (1) forgery, (2) deception or lying or untruthfulness, (3) corruption of the original text by addition, change, or diminution—especially by change.

If, for instance, a certain book purported to be written by a close friend of the Duke of Windsor—let us say by George Dyson—and to give a full account of Edward VIII.'s brief span of life as king; if, after careful investigation it were found that no such person as George Dyson ever existed or that George Dyson, a personal friend of the Duke, never wrote a single line of the book, then we should at once cast aside such a work as a mere fairy tale or, what is worse, a forgery.

Secondly, even though it is certain that a certain author or authoress, e.g., Maria Monk, wrote such a book, if it is also clearly established that such writer is either deceived or deceiving, i.e., either a lunatic or a liar, then no reasonable person will accept the statements or charges contained in such a discredited production.

Thirdly, even though we are certain that Gerald McIvor wrote an account of his three years' sojourn in Madagascar, and that he was a reliable writer, still if it be proved that a great deal of his original writing has been cut out, that what was kept has been constantly changed, and that much fiction, or untruth, has been added, then no thinking person will swallow the account as given in the present work.

But every reasonable person must accept a work as a true historical document, or a faithful or correct record of past events, if it can be clearly proved (1) that the work under consideration was written by the author to whom it is attributed, (2) that this author is reliable, i.e., neither deceived as to the events he recorded nor deceptive or untruthful in narrating them (that is, that he had evidence or at least true knowledge of such events and faithfully or truthfully chronicled them), and (3) that the work he wrote has not been substantially corrupted, i.e., that the record he wrote is substantially entire or intact. I say substantially, for the reliability of a work is not affected if some sentences have undergone slight changes which preserve the original meaning, if some minor or unimportant phrase has happened to drop out, etc.

Now, when the New Testament is submitted to these tests, it is abundantly clear to every well-disposed and right-thinking person that the books it contains are reliable historical documents. The Epistles, of course, are chiefly doctrinal instructions and moral exhortations, but they obviously contain many historical facts concerning Christ. The Apocalypse is essentially a prophetic book, though it, too, contains a certain narrative of Christ and His work. But we are concerned especially with the four Gospels, which are historical narratives of Christ's earthly life.

HISTORICAL VALUE OF NEW TESTAMENT WRITINGS

Let me quote from an excellent work on the matter I am explaining. The title of the work is "The Gospels—Fact, Myth, or Legend," and the author is the well-known scholar and writer, J. P. Arendzen, Ph.D., D.D., M.A. Cantab. I shall gladly lend you this book. You need not read the whole of it, although this would be very beneficial if you had the time. In fact, I shall not ask you to read the book at all, though you are welcome to it. Listen to this passage, which refers to the Epistles:

"Let us take the collection of letters first. Practically no modern scholar who teaches at any University or recognized centre of learning, whether he be Christian or not, and who is acknowledged to be an expert in these matters, denies that the bulk of these letters, nine-tenths of them, was written between the years 50 and 90 A.D. of the first century, and three fourths between 50 and 65 A.D. . . The only letter which is still impugned by some scholars as perhaps a second-century forgery is the short epistle known as Second Peter" (p. 2). I shall not here prove the genuineness of the second Epistle of St. Peter, for we shall not require that document in the chats which immediately follow.

As for the Gospels, the proofs of their reliability as historical records is simply overwhelming. If you are fond of reading and have the leisure, I shall lend you a pamphlet on "Bible Quizzes to a Street Preacher" and "Radio Replies," Volumes I, II and III, by Fathers Rumble and Carty. But again I am not asking you to do so, for our chats alone will give you a sufficient knowledge and sufficient proof of the Catholic religion.

We might summarise thus the detailed proofs of the trustworthiness of the Gospels:

I. **General Argument:** Every scholar (I mean every genuine historian) admits that by the end of the second century the four Gospels were received and admitted throughout Christendom as genuine, truthful, intact records of the life and teaching of Christ, written by the four authors to whom they were ascribed: Matthew, Mark, Luke, and John. In fact, it is historically certain that the Gospels were thus well known amongst Christians during the first part of the second century. But, in the light of all the circumstances of the time, it is a sheer impossibility to explain such unreserved acceptance of these four documents unless they were reliable records of the events they narrate.

The Apostles, who sealed their faith with their blood, would never have allowed spurious or untruthful records of Christianity to be circulated; converts from Judaism would never have given them the same authority as the books of the Old Testament; the Jews who attacked the Christian religion would have disproved the reliability of such documents, as they could so easily have done in the case of forgeries and myths; pagan scholars of the first rank would never have admitted them, much less put complete faith in them; heretics—those who broke away from the Christian Church—would have repudiated them; Christians would not have died in thousands rather than deny them.

II. **Particular Argument:** Testimony of early writers. I shall not weary you, my dear inquirer, with a string of quotations. You may, if you wish, read them carefully in the works mentioned, which I shall gladly lend you. But let me give you **one very striking testimony.**

ST. IRENAEUS

St. John the Apostle and Evangelist had amongst his disciples a distinguished pupil named Polycarp, who later laid down his life for the Christian faith. Polycarp instructed Irenaeus, who was born in Asia Minor and lived there in his younger days. Irenaeus, after leaving his native country, spent some time in Rome and became Bishop of Lyons (in France). He is admittedly one of the great scholars of the second century and one of the most illustrious martyrs. His testimony, then, regarding the Gospels, is surely of immense value. This is what Irenaeus wrote in his well-known work, "Against Heresies":

"Matthew wrote a Gospel for the Jews in their own language, while Peter and Paul were preaching and establishing the Church at Rome. After their departure Mark also, the disciple and interpreter of Peter, handed down to us in writing the information which Peter had given. And Luke, the follower of Paul, wrote out the Gospel which Paul used to preach. Later John, the disciple of the Lord, who had reclined on His breast, published his Gospel during his sojourn in Asia Minor."

GOSPELS AND CLASSICS COMPARED

We must remember that printing was not invented for long centuries after the first appearance of the Gospels, and that they had to be transcribed as had all written works of the time. Although the original copies and, indeed, the first transcribed copies of religious and secular works have perished, faithfully-made copies continued. Now, although the earliest manuscripts we have of the Latin and Greek classics, which are accepted as genuine by classical scholars, date from the eighth or ninth centuries, our manuscripts of the Gospels go back to the fourth and fifth centuries, and even earlier. Again, the earliest references to Caesar's Commentaries on the Gallic War are not found till one hundred years after Caesar's death, and then only in the writings of Plutarch and Suetonius, whereas there are abundant references to the four Gospels and their authors within a much shorter time from the death of the writers. If certain prejudiced critics applied to the Greek and Latin classics the same method as they do in examining the Gospels, we should have to say a long farewell to our cherished Greek and Latin classical works (probably to the great joy of many a high school student).

Nothing but pride or prejudice or mental blindness can prevent anyone who studies the matter from accepting the New Testament as a collection of genuine, truthful, intact historical documents.

CHAPTER IV.

THE DIVINITY OF CHRIST

IN our last chapter I concluded by saying that I would quote from the New Testament in this talk. I shall do this in order to prove that Jesus Christ is the Son of God; that He is truly God, Who became man for love of us; that He is the God-Man.

I would ask you to read, in your leisure moments, the four Gospels, which you will find in the New Testament I gave you. In this chat I shall single out some prominent passages which clearly show that Christ is God.

No one (I mean no person in his right senses, or at least no person who has a shred of historical knowledge) denies that Christ is a true historic figure; that He lived and died in Palestine at the beginning of the Christian era; that, in fact, the letters B.C. and A.D. (Anno Domini—the Year of the Lord), which are universally used, proclaim the historic existence of Jesus Christ. But, while Christians—at least all genuine Christians—firmly believe that Christ is God as well as man, unbelievers—rationalists, agnostics, and atheists—hold that Jesus was simply an outstanding personality, a great man, a wonderful teacher of what is noble and good. Even no Jew who lays claim to any scholarship doubts the existence of Christ. Indeed, it is a sad fact that since the year 88 A.D. the Jews have added to their most solemn prayer a bitter curse against the followers of Jesus of Nazareth, thus reluctantly testifying to both His existence and His influence on men. Rabbi Stephen S. Wise, prominent Jewish Liberal of New York City, proclaimed Jesus to be "the radiant Jewish teacher of Palestine" (January 3, 1926). I was in America at the time, and I well remember the brilliant and beautiful open letter which Dr. David Goldstein, a distinguished convert from Judaism to Christianity (to the very fullness of Catholicity), wrote on that occasion to Rabbi Wise. In this letter Dr. Goldstein conclusively proves the Divinity of Christ. Here is one striking passage:

"If, as you aver, Jesus attained to heavenly heights —if He lived divinely as a man—He must necessarily have been the personification of truth, since the adherence to truth is the test of any man's integrity. What, then, my dear Rabbi Wise? Is it too much to expect that yourself and your admirers should be willing to listen to and also to accept the statements of so sublime a Jewish teacher as to who in truth He says He is?"

That is just the point. Since, as Rabbi Wise admits, and with him prominent rationalists like Lecky and Renan, Christ, the true, historical Christ, was a man of most eminent integrity and holiness, it follows that we **must** accept what He says of Himself. If He declares, explicitly or implicitly, that He is God, then we are bound to render Him divine homage. If He claims to be God, and we are unwilling to admit such claims, then not only could we not proclaim Him to be a radiant teacher or a man of sublime integrity, but we should be obliged to regard Him as a tremendous impostor. Once we admit the character of Jesus as portrayed by Lecky, Renan, Wise, and others outside the pale of Christianity, we must, if we are logical, go one step further and acknowledge Christ as **God,** for He clearly claimed to be divine, to be the **Son of** God, to be God Himself. Let us consider Christ's own words and acts.

CHRIST'S OWN CLAIMS

1 **He teaches as God.** You have heard that it was said to them of old . . . but I say to you. . . ." (Matt. V., 21). Here He teaches and **legislates as God.** "Heaven and earth shall pass away, but my words shall not pass away" (Luke VI., 40).

2. He claims to be the **Supreme Judge** of mankind, and gives, as the reason for rewarding the charitable: "As often as you have done it to one of these, the least of my little ones, you have done it to Me" (Matt. XXV.).

3. He forgives sin **by His own authority.** (Mark II.; Luke VII.)

4. He prescribes **faith in Himself** and **love for Himself** as conditions of salvation (Matt. X. and XVIII.).

5. Any work, He declares, that is done **for His sake,** will be eternally rewarded (Mark X.; Matt. V., X., XIX.).

6. He promises His disciples **His own abiding presence and help** (Matt. XI., XVIII., XXVIII.).

7. He receives homage as **the natural Son of God** (Matt. XVI.).

8. In prescribing the form of baptism, **He places Himself on an equality with the Father** (Matt. XXVIII.).

9. The chief scope of the fourth Gospel, whose reliability cannot be reasonably questioned, is to show that Christ is truly God. From the opening passage,

"In the beginning was the Word, and the Word was with God, and **the Word was God**," to the final words, "But these things have been written that you may believe that Jesus is the Son of God," the Divinity of Jesus Christ is clearly taught and insisted on by the Beloved Disciple, John the Evangelist. In this Gospel, too, the claims made by Christ Himself are narrated in a striking manner, and His divinity is expressed as clearly as possible in the discourses which are recorded of Him. He claims to be the **only-begotten Son of God** (III.); He declares that He works together with the Father (V.); He claims the power **to raise whom He wishes from the dead** (V.); He teaches that He is **one with the Father** (X.); that whoever sees Him sees the Father (XIV.); that He is **eternal** (VIII.); that He is **the resurrection and the life;** the way, the truth, and the life (XI., XIV.); He accepts the **adoration** of the man whose sight He had restored (X.), and of St. Thomas, who exclaimed: "My Lord and my God" (XX.).

THE MIRACLES OF JESUS

A miracle is an external action or fact which shows forth God's almighty power and infinite knowledge; or a fact or deed, perceptible by us, that is produced outside or above the order of all nature, i.e., an external action or fact that only God can do or perform. A man may throw a stone into the air; that is not a miracle because the natural power of man performs the act. An immense ship is blown up by shells or torpedoes; that is not a miracle, because it is effected by means devised by man and fashioned from the natural forces and material of Nature. But no created agent can raise a dead man to life, such an act is beyond the forces or order of the whole of created Nature; such an action can be

23

performed by God alone; it is an external act, because it is visible to man; it is a divine act, because only God's omnipotence can effect it. And therefore it is a miracle.

But, my dear friend, I am not giving you a talk on miracles. If you desire more information about them, I shall gladly lend you some literature. And later on, if you have time, I shall tell you all about two visits I paid to Lourdes and the study I made of the records kept there, which show beyond doubt that many miracles have been wrought at that world-famed shrine. But let us consider the miracles worked by Jesus Christ.

In the presence of many witnesses of every rank in life; in various places and at different times; on behalf of all kinds of sufferers and persons in need, Christ worked miracle after miracle during the three years of His public life. The miracles performed by Christ are genuine historical facts which no person of **normal intelligence, unbiased mind, and upright heart** can fail to accept.

Christ, by an act of His will, gave sight to the blind, hearing to the deaf, speech to the dumb, health to the sick; He quelled the storm raging on the sea of Tiberias, multiplied a few loaves and fishes to feed thousands of people, and caused the rabble to fall prostrate in the Garden of Olives; He even raised the dead to life. So striking and public was the resurrection of Lazarus, who had already been buried, that the Jewish leaders wished to kill Lazarus, as if (remarks St. Augustine) He Who had already raised Lazarus from the dead could not raise him again if he were killed!

All these miracles Christ worked by His own power, as is shown in the Gospels and expressly declared by Himself. And He claimed that these divine works were performed in testimony of His doctrine. Hence that doctrine must be divine. And one of the cardinal points of His teaching, the very fundamental truth of His doctrine, is that He is truly the Son of God, the only-begotten Son of God, one with the Father, the eternal One. Thus, both because of the miracles themselves and because of the doctrine to which they give unmistakably divine testimony, we must acknowledge Christ as God.

While dealing with the miracles of Christ, I could treat also of His prophecies, His accurate foretelling of future events known to God alone. The argument drawn from a consideration of His prophecies is akin to the proof derived from His miracles.

CHRIST'S GLORIOUS RESURRECTION

The resurrection of Christ may be termed His supreme miracle. He clearly foretold that He would be put to death (by crucifixion) and that He would rise again on the third day. Even His enemies were aware of this prophecy and set a guard over the tomb in which Jesus, who had certainly died on the Cross, was laid. But Christ came forth gloriously living from the tomb and was seen by the Apostles and hundreds of other witnesses during the forty days that followed. His resurrection is the crowning proof of His divinity, as His death on the Cross is an evident proof of His mortal human nature. Our simple Catechism rightly says: "By dying on the Cross Christ showed Himself a real mortal man, and by raising Himself from the dead He proved Himself God."

TESTIMONY OF THE MARTYRS

This chat, my dear friend, has been long enough. I have condensed the chief proofs that Christ is truly

God, and these proofs are abundantly clear and convincing. In conclusion, however, I would stress the fact that the Apostles and others who had lived during Christ's life and heard Him gladly shed their blood to confess His divinity. Would they have given up all that the world holds dear, even life itself, unless they were absolutely convinced that Christ was God and rightly claimed their whole-hearted love and service. Since the days of the Apostles millions of Christians have also joyfully sealed with their blood their faith in the Divinity of Jesus Christ. May you also, my dear inquirer, not only recognise Christ as God, but also submit your mind and heart to the teachings of the Church which He founded. Of Christ's one Church I shall tell you in our next chat.

CHAPTER V.

THE TRUE CHURCH

WHILE Christ lived on this earth, He, the Incarnate Son of God, "the Way, the Truth, and the Life," taught men. During the three years of His public life He proclaimed God's revealed truth—Divine Revelation. This He did in the Jewish synagogues (which were like smaller churches), in the temple (which was like a glorious cathedral), at the lakeside, on the mountain, in desert places, and from Peter's barque. At times He discoursed with but a few persons, at other times in the presence of great crowds, and again to one person at a time. But He almost always had with Him His twelve chosen Apostles. To these He often explained in private what He had taught in public.

Since Christ was not to remain always on this earth, in His visible presence, how was His doctrine to be perpetuated, or taught forever, on this earth? The answer is that He instituted a teaching body of men, a living college of teachers, who were appointed by Him to make known His teaching till the end of time. In other words, He founded a church to carry on, until the end of the world, His own work of teaching and sanctifying (making holy) mankind.

HOW MANY CHURCHES ARE THERE?

But, my dear friend, you may ask: How many churches are there? To me, you may say, there seems no end of churches or religious denominations. I have heard of the Church of England, the Methodists, the Lutherans, the Presbyterians, the Mormons, the Baptists, the Salvation Army, the Witnesses of Jehovah, and other denominations. And, of course, I am aware of the existence of the Catholic Church, or, as some call it, the Church of Rome. This is all bewildering to an inquirer.

To your inquiry in this matter, I would answer that you may, if you wish, speak of those different **churches**, though I would prefer to call all of them, with one exception, just religious denominations or sects. However, let the term **church** pass for the present. Then I shall say that there is **only one true church.** For the moment you need not ask which is that Church, but I am sure you will readily admit that all the churches or denominations you have mentioned cannot be equally true. Why, there is hopeless contradiction in their teachings or tenets or doctrines. Suppose you were teaching a class of children and you gave them the simple question: How many dozen are there in one hundred and twenty? And suppose one child said five, another six, a third fourteen, and a fourth ten, would you tell the class that all the answers were right? Certainly not, for, if the child who answered ten is right, the others are evidently wrong.

Again, if you asked two boys whether gold is more precious than brass, and one boy replied yes while the other answered no, would you tell the boys that both were right?

Well, just as we cannot admit contrary or contradictory answers to the same question, so we cannot admit that religious bodies which are quite opposed in their teachings and principles are all equally true.

Our reason tells us that there can be but one true religion or one true church. Only if we admit the absurd statement that there can be a dozen true Gods, or a dozen different Christs, can we hold that there are a dozen true churches. Besides, Christ always spoke of the Church in the singular number—**my Church, the Church.**

Some well-meaning, though illogical, persons say that, after all, we are but taking different roads to the same destination. Now, if you wished to travel from San Francisco to Los Angeles, and one person told you to go north, while another bade you go south, would you accept both directions as equally good, as equally true? Obviously not. But how, I ask, is it that people can be so logical or reasonable in ordinary life—in school, in business, in motoring, etc.—and yet admit, or unquestioningly accept, such absurd principles and statements in the matter of religion?

WHICH IS THE TRUE CHURCH?

Well, my dear friend, you may say: Yes, all that you say is quite reasonable; there clearly can be but one true church; but how am I to recognize it or "sort it out" from the medley around me?

I shall answer your question in the words of a little child. I have often put your question to our school-children and the little ones have frequently replied: The Catholic Church is the one true Church, because all the other churches were made by men, but only the Catholic Church was made by Jesus Christ.

Let us now examine this simple answer. Were all the other churches made by mere men? A knowledge of history will convince you that such is the case. Let us first of all take the Anglican Church, which seems to be the largest religious body in many English-speaking countries, though not in all of them. What is the origin of this religious body? Undoubtedly it was not in existence before the sixteenth century. When Henry VIII. ascended the throne, the whole of England was Catholic (or, as some would say, Roman Catholic). But Henry wanted to put away his lawful wife, Catherine of Aragon, and marry Anne Boleyn. He appealed to the Pope, the recognized Head of the Church, for a divorce, or an annulment of his marriage with Catherine. This, of course, the Pope could not grant. So Henry declared himself Head of the Church in England, set up his own ecclesiastical tribunal, got the desired divorce, and married Anne. The "Act of Supremacy," which declared the King Head of the Church in England, is known to every student of English history. And the "Oath of Supremacy," which Sir Thomas More, like other faithful Catholics, refused to take, though his heroism cost his life, is also well known. That "Bluff King Hal" is the founder and father of the Anglican Church cannot be denied by anyone who squarely faces the facts of history.

The Lutheran Church or religion was founded in Germany by Martin Luther, who is called the real father of Protestantism. The Presbyterian religion owes its origin to Calvin, and, in Scotland, to his disciple, John Knox. The Methodist Church traces its beginning to John Wesley and his brother Charles. And nowadays we have still newer religions. Brigham Young, Mrs. Eddy, "Judge" Rutherford, and a score of others have gone their own ways, starting their own peculiar denominations.

We can tell the name of the founder of every non-Catholic denomination, the country in which it sprang up, the year of its beginning, and the circumstances of its origin. But, when we turn to our separated brethren and ask them to answer the same questions regarding the Catholic Church, they are compelled to remain silent or else to admit that the Catholic Church was founded nineteen centuries ago by Jesus Christ. No wonder that scholarly Englishman, saintly churchman, and distinguished convert from Anglicanism, John Henry Newman, exclaimed: "To be deep in history is to cease to be a Protestant."

In our next chat, I shall show how Christ established His Church and shall prove that this Church is surely the Church of Rome, or, as it is more correctly called, the Catholic Church.

REMOVING SOME MISGIVINGS

But before closing let me, in a truly friendly spirit, remove one or two misgivings.

First, we do not pass judgment on the conscience of our non-Catholic friends. They have been born and brought up in their respective denominations and cannot be held responsible for what Henry VIII. or Martin Luther or Calvin or John Knox did. Many of them are in good faith and are leading edifying Christian lives. Certainly we Catholics have no wish to quarrel about religion. Religion is too sacred a thing to quarrel about. But it is of supreme importance and should, therefore, be carefully and prayerfully examined.

Secondly, the only reason why we are desirous of showing our separated brethren the truth of the Catholic faith is that we love them and wish them to share with us the blessings of the Church established by Jesus Christ. We invite them to enter the grand kingdom instituted by our loving Redeemer in order that they may be as rich as we are in the gifts of God (without any merit on our part) in this life, and as blessed and happy as we hope to be in eternity.

And now, my dear inquirer, while awaiting further instruction, pray fervently that God may give you light to see His holy will and strength to accomplish it. I recommend you to say earnestly that beautiful hymn composed by Newman and now sung throughout the English-speaking world:

Lead, Kindly Light, amid the encircling gloom,
Lead Thou me on.

The night is dark, and I am far from home;
Lead Thou me on.

Keep Thou my feet; I do not ask to see

The distant scene. One step enough for me.

CHAPTER VI.

THE TRUE CHURCH (continued)

IN order to show that the Catholic Church was founded by Jesus Christ, we must go back to the Gospels, about which I told you in our third chat. We shall abstract from their inspired character, about which you will be told later on, and shall consider them merely as historical documents, whose reliability, as I have shown, cannot be reasonably questioned.

In the last chat I mentioned the Apostles, who were Christ's constant companions during His public life on earth. Now, the office of these chosen disciples was, as the Gospels clearly show, to go forth after Christ's ascension and teach all men the truths that had been revealed to themselves. In this ministry they were not to be left to themselves, for thus either they or their successors could fall into error in their teaching and thus lead mankind astray. No, Christ, Who is Infinite Wisdom Incarnate, would not allow His revelation to be thus corrupted and His work undone, and so He endowed His teaching body—the Apostolic college and their successors till the end of time—with **infallibility.** That big word is often confused with another big word, **impeccability.** The latter term means freedom from the power of sinning. A person is **impeccable** if he cannot sin. Jesus Christ could not sin, for He is a Divine Person. But we poor mortals—even the chosen Apostles—are all sinners. The Apostles had to work out their salvation like us. We do not, as some people imagine, claim impeccability for the Pope. However, let me leave the Papacy for a future chat.

CHRIST PROMISED THE CHURCH INFALLIBILITY

Infallibility means freedom from teaching error; it means that, through God's protection and guidance, the Apostles and their successors must, in their official teaching, set forth the very teaching of Christ without addition, diminution (or lessening), change, or corruption. Christ emphatically, solemnly, and repeatedly guaranteed that His Church would never fall into error—that the living authority He established to teach mankind would be gifted with freedom from error in its official teaching, so that His Church would live on through the ages unchanged and unchangeable, uncorrupted and incorruptible, unconquered and unconquerable. Thus the oldest church, which is admittedly the Catholic Church (which, at any rate, is admitted to have been in existence centuries before Protestantism), must be the true Church for the simple reason that the Church Christ founded could not change. But I must develop and explain this simple, convincing argument. Let us go to the Gospels and see how plainly and emphatically Christ promised that the Church He founded would never err.

1. "He that heareth you," declared Christ to the Apostles, "heareth Me" (Luke 10:16). Could this be said if it were possible for them to teach error? No, for in that case those who heard the Apostles would be listening not to Christ and His message of truth, but to erring men teaching false doctrines.

2. In addressing Simon, whose name He changed to **Peter** (which means **rock**), Jesus also made a solemn promise regarding the Church: "I say to thee that thou

34

art Peter, and upon this rock I will build My Church, and the gates of hell shall not prevail against it" (Matt. 16:18). These words express a clear guarantee that the Church will never be allowed by its Divine Founder to teach error; that Christ will ever watch over and guide it, so that the powers of darkness and error may never prevail against or overcome it.

3. The fourteenth chapter of St. John's Gospel also contains a plain guarantee that the Church of Christ would never fall into error, for it would be blessed with the abiding presence of the Spirit of Truth. Our Redeemer made it quite clear that the Spirit of Truth would remain with the teaching body (the Apostles and their successors) not merely for a few centuries, so that the Church would afterwards fall a prey to false doctrines and remain in that state for hundreds of years until Martin Luther should appear to enlighten it, but right on till the end of time—**for ever.** Here are Our Lord's own words: "I will ask the Father, and He will give you another Comforter, the Spirit of Truth, that He may abide with you for ever. . . . The Comforter, the Holy Ghost, whom the Father will send in My name, will teach you all things, and bring all things to your mind, whatsoever I shall have said to you" (vv. 16-26).

4. From the fact that those who refuse to believe the teaching of Christ's Apostles and their successors are threatened with everlasting punishment, we must infer that such teaching could never be wrong, for how could God, Who is infinitely just, condemn anyone refusing to believe a false doctrine? Our Saviour imposes on men the same duty of assent to the teaching of the Church as to His own: "Go ye into the whole world and preach the Gospel to every creature," He said to the Apostles—words which obviously referred

also to their successors, for the Apostles, whose span of life was comparatively short and whose power of travel was necessarily limited, could not personally complete this mission. Mark well what follows: "He that believeth and is baptised shall be saved, but he that believeth not shall be condemned" (Mark 16:16).

5. Before ascending to heaven, Jesus gave His final commission to the Apostles, which commission manifestly refers also to their lawful successors, for the Apostles could not personally teach all nations, and, besides, Christ speaks of His assistance **till the end of the world.** He solemnly bade His Apostles go forth and teach all nations all the doctrines He had entrusted or made known to them, and at the same time He gave an emphatic assurance or guarantee that, in this ministry of teaching, He would be in their midst, assisting them and guiding them, not merely for a few centuries, but **even until the end of the world.** Could there be a clearer promise that the Church would be always preserved from error in its teaching—that it would always enjoy infallibility? Study Christ's words as recorded by St. Matthew: "Jesus coming spoke to them, saying: 'All power is given to Me in heaven and on earth. Going, therefore, teach ye all nations, baptising them in the name of the Father and of the Son and of the Holy Ghost, teaching them to observe all things whatsoever I have commanded you; and lo! I am with you all days, even unto the end of the world' (28:20).

THE APOSTLES CLAIMED INFALLIBILITY

From all the passages I have quoted, my dear inquirer, it is abundantly plain that Christ gave a solemn assurance that His Church would never fall into error; that it would ever teach the very truths He had committed to it; that, in a word, it would always be infallible. The Apostles, of course,, were fully aware of this, and they explicitly claimed infallibility in their teaching.

1. They call the Holy Ghost a fellow witness of the truths they proclaim to men: "We are witnesses of those things, and the Holy Ghost, whom God hath given to all that obey Him" (Acts 5:32). Again: "It hath seemed good to the Holy Ghost and to us" (ibid. 15:28).

2. St. Paul claims that the teaching of the Apostles is the very word of God: "Our exhortation was not of error, nor of uncleanness, nor in deceit; but as we were approved of God that the Gospel should be committed to us, even so we speak not as pleasing men, but God, who proveth our hearts" (1 Thess. II., 3). And again: "When you had received of us the word of the hearing of God, you received it not as the word of men, but (as it truly is) the word of God, Who worketh in you that you have believed" (ibid. 13).

3. St. Paul is so confident that the Church cannot err that He regards it as a divine pillar and foundation of truth: "The Church of the living God, the pillar and the ground of truth" (1 Tim. 3:15).

From what has been proved it follows that the Church founded by Christ simply could not change its doctrine. Hence the Church of the third century taught the same doctrines as the Church of the Apostles; the Church of the sixth century the same as the Church of the third; the Church of the sixteenth century the same as the Church of the sixth, of the third, and of the Apostles.

Yet, in the sixteenth century, when the whole of Christendom was Catholic, or, as some would prefer to say, Roman Catholic (with the exception of the

Greeks, who had finally broken away in the fifteenth century, but who still believed practically every Catholic doctrine), Martin Luther and Company rose up and denied doctrine after doctrine of the Universal Church, setting up their own men-made systems of religion.

To say that Luther, Calvin, Henry VIII., Cranmer, John Knox, and other sixteenth century and later rebels against the Universal Church were right, is not only to admit that contradictions can be true, but it is also to utter the implicit blasphemy that Christ did not keep His solemn promises—that he who heard the Apostles and their successors did not hear Christ; that the Spirit of Truth did not remain with the teachers of the Church for ever; that Christ did not stay with his teaching body all days; that the Church is not the pillar and the ground of truth.

Once we accept the Gospels as trustworthy historical documents, we must admit that Christ is divine and that the Catholic Church is the one Church founded by Him. For the doctrine of the Catholic Church in the sixteenth century must have been identical with the doctrine of the Church of the Apostles, and the teaching of the Catholic Church of the twentieth century must be the same as that of the Church of the sixteenth century.

TESTIMONY OF LORD MACAULAY

The Catholic Church will live on until the end of time, ever guarded by her Divine Founder; ever blessed with the presence of the Spirit of Truth; ever triumphing over error, ever shining before the world as a divine institution, as the one true Church, the Church of Jesus Christ.

No one can consider Lord Macaulay prejudiced in favour of the Catholic Church. Yet he wrote of her: "She may still exist in undiminished vigor when some traveller from New Zealand shall, in the midst of a vast solitude, take his stand on a broken arch of London Bridge to sketch the ruins of St. Paul's."

Let me now, my dear friend, in closing our chat, narrate a little story. A Catholic, a Protestant, and a Jew once had a friendly argument as to which is the true religion. They could argue for hours (and often did) without the slightest sign of a quarrel. And always they parted the best of friends. On the occasion to which I allude the three had a very long discussion. At last the Jew said: "I'll sum up the whole situation. If the Messiah has not come, my religion is right. If the Messiah has come, the religion of our friend the Catholic is right. But, whether the Messiah has come or not, the religion of our friend the Protestant is wrong."

CHAPTER VII.

THE MARKS OF THE TRUE CHURCH

THERE are certain marks or visible attributes with which the Church of Christ is endowed. Our reason tells us that, if God the Son made man instituted a Church for the salvation of mankind, it must have these properties, and, when we study the Gospels and the other New Testament writings, that conviction is confirmed. I shall single out the chief marks which characterize the Church established by Jesus Christ. They are four in number: unity, catholicity, apostolicity, and holiness. Let us consider each.

CHRIST'S CHURCH MUST BE ONE

Of course, there can be only one Church of Christ. But at present, in speaking of **unity** or **oneness**, we mean that the same doctrines must be taught throughout the Church and that the same doctrines must be believed by all the members of the Church without exception; that the same sacraments must be administered everywhere in the Church, the self-same sacrifice offered, and the same supreme authority obeyed. Only when these conditions are fulfilled, can we have true unity in a church. Now, anyone who gives even a passing glance at non-Catholic denominations (or, if you wish, non-Catholic churches) must see that no such unity is found in any of them; that, in fact, such unity is unattainable by them in their present condition.

PRIVATE JUDGMENT RENDERS UNITY IMPOSSIBLE

No Protestant Church claims infallibility. Yet without an infallible authority doctrinal unity is an impossibility. And the principle of **private judgment,** according to which each one takes his own meaning out of Scripture, which he regards as the only source of God's revelation, makes it a sheer impossibility to have anything even approaching doctrinal unity in the true sense of the expression. This is evident; and so I need not dwell on it, although I could give you many instances to prove it.

Even in the Church of England, with the official Book of Common Prayer and with Bishops, there is hopeless division. There we see the High Church, the Broad Church, and the Low Church. There we see a man like Bishop Barnes, of Birmingham, teaching what is the contradiction of traditional Anglicanism and even the contradiction of the fundamental tenets of Christianity, yet still holding his office as Anglican Bishop. Just ask any member of the Anglican Church: What doctrines exactly must one hold in order to be a member of your church, and what doctrines exactly may he reject without ceasing to be an Anglican? I have never received a reply to that question. But one young man, to whom I put that, amongst other questions, and who was contemplating taking Anglican Orders, ended by becoming a Catholic. I may say, in passing, that the following were the questions I put to him, adding that, of course, he might consult his own minister:—

(1) What exactly must I believe in order to be an Anglican, and what may I reject without ceasing to be an Anglican?

(2) If a dissension or controversy arises in the Church of England on important, fundamental, vital

matters, who has authority to give a final, definite, irrevocable decision?

(3) By what authority did a group of Englishmen in the sixteenth century change the formula of Ordination that had come down from time immemorial, and draw up a formulary of their own?

(4) Do you consider the Edwardine Ordinal of 1552 a sufficient means or formula for the valid consecration of a bishop and the valid ordination of a priest?

(5) If so, why did the Anglican Church evidently **correct** the Ordinal in 1662?

(6) If the correction was **essential** (as I certainly maintain it was), and "priests" had been ordained and "bishops" consecrated **invalidly** in the Anglican Church for one hundred and ten years, don't you think that your church no longer had any priests or bishops and that it was too late to rectify the Ordinal.

Now, my dear inquirer, I do not expect you to go into those questions yet; I just mentioned this matter in passing, though it pertains to the subject we are chatting over. Perhaps, however, you are not now surprised that the young man to whom I put those questions decided not to take Orders in the Anglican Church, but to become a Catholic. As for **Orders, I** shall explain that matter to you in due time. At present I am treating of **unity.**

MARVELLOUS UNITY IN THE CHURCH OF ROME

In the Church of Rome (I use this expression because I have presently to prove that it alone is **catholic),** we behold a wondrous unity of doctrine, worship, and government. In whatever matters—and they are numerous—the Church has lifted up her infallible voice and laid down irrevocable decisions, from the days of the first General Council of Bishops to the present time, there is no room in the Church of Rome for two opinions. You may go to a Catholic school-child in Mexico, to a Catholic priest in Japan, to a Catholic old lady in America, to a Catholic young man in Ireland or England or Scotland, to a Catholic Bishop in France or Spain or Germany, to a Child of Mary in Italy or Australia—you may approach a Catholic of any age or sex or condition in any country throughout the whole world—and ask: Should we pray for the dead? Is the Mass a sacrifice? Ought we to honor· and invoke the Blessed Virgin? How are we to get our sins forgiven? Is Baptism necessary for salvation? What is the Blessed Eucharist? Who is the visible Head of the Church? **Always and everywhere you will receive the very same answer.**

The wondrous unity of the Church of Rome is **in itself,** apart from the historical arguments I gave in our previous chat, a convincing proof of the divinity of our Church, for such extraordinary unity amongst over four hundred millions of people who differ in language, nationality,· and political interests, yet unite perfectly in believing and professing the same doctrines, receiving the same sacraments, offering the same sacrifice, and obeying the same visible Head, is truly a supernatural phenomenon—a stupendous, marvellous reality that can be explained only as coming from God.

CATHOLICITY

The word **catholic** means **universal**—belonging to every nation, international, supranational. **Catholic** means pertaining to **every age** or century and to **every country** or race. It is the opposite of **national, and** hence any religious organization that has a national sovereign—an earthly king—as its head and is also practically restricted, as regards its membership, to the country or empire over which that king holds sway, must say good-bye to any claim to catholicity. Therefore, the Church of England is decidedly not Catholic. To apply to it the term **Anglo-Catholic** is to unite two contradictory or opposing things and is as logical as to talk of **fried ice-cream!** Likewise, the other various Protestant denominations must be excluded from any logical claim to Catholicity, for Lutherans are confined chiefly to Germans and people of German descent, Methodists chiefly to a certain portion or certain portions of the English-speaking people, Presbyterians especially to Scots and those of Scottish descent, and so on. Besides, not one non-Catholic (or "non-Roman") denomination belongs to **every century**, for Protestantism sprang up, as I have shown, in the sixteenth century. And the Greek Church broke away in the eighth century, returned to re-union with Rome later on, and finally broke off in the fifteenth century; and, besides, it comprises only some oriental races, especially Greeks.

But the great Church over which the Bishop of Rome exercises jurisdiction is alone truly catholic, for it comprises more than four hundred million members, outnumbering all Protestants combined, and probably Protestants and Greeks combined. It embraces people of every nation—English and Germans, French and Italians, Spaniards and Irish, Americans and Australians, Greeks and Jugo-Slavs, Chinese and Indians, Japanese and Arabs, and it also extends back to every century from the time of Christ.

At times we hear the expression **Roman Catholic.** And some Anglicans say that they use **Anglo-Catholic** in a similar sense, qualifying **Catholic** by **Anglo.** But there is a tremendous difference between the use of the qualifying particle in the two cases, for **Anglo** denotes the nationality—the national character of the church—whereas **Roman** has nothing to do with the nationality of Catholics, but simply denotes that the head of the Catholic Church, which **embraces all nations,** is the Bishop of Rome. Rome is to the Catholic Church what the centre of a circle is to the circumference. Roman Catholic, then, and Catholic are synonymous; that is, they have exactly the same meaning.

APOSTOLICITY AND HOLINESS

I must not make our chat too long for you, my dear inquirer, and so I shall speak but briefly of the two other marks of the Church. From what I said in our previous chats it is evident that the Catholic Church, dating back, not to Luther or Calvin or Henry VIII., but to our Saviour Himself, who founded it on the Apostles, is alone truly apostolic. Besides, we can point to the long line of Roman Pontiffs, uninterrupted from Peter to Pius XII., thus showing true apostolic succession.

As regards holiness, we do not claim that all Catholics are leading exemplary lives or deny that many non-Catholics are personally holy. When we say that the Catholic Church is eminently holy, we mean that her doctrines are heavenly and her moral code so sublime as to be the most exalted that the human race has known. In fact, it is sometimes urged against her that her exposition of the divine law in regard to purity, marriage, justice, and self-denial is too rigid, and that her own discipline is too exacting. By the holiness of the Church we mean also that she provides her members with the most effective means of attaining a very high standard of sanctity, and she has actu ally produced extraordinary holiness in the lives of countless souls within her bosom. We mean also that her teaching and means of sanctification have caused to blossom forth, down through the centuries, institutions that bear upon their countenances the seal of heavenly holiness—religious Orders, orphanages, hospitals, homes for the fallen and aged, schools and colleges, missionary societies, organizations consecrated to relief of the poor, and countless holy undertakings.

One who carefully and prayerfully studies the Church of Rome and considers her unity, catholicity, apostolicity, and holiness, must spontaneously bow to her and accept her teachings as the doctrines of Jesus Christ made known to fallen men through his infallible mouthpiece.

CHAPTER VIII

THE PAPACY

SO far, my dear inquirer, I have proved to you from mere reason that there is an eternal, intelligent, infinite Being whom we call God, and that He may, if He choose, reveal truths to mankind. I have shown that the New Testament is a collection of trustworthy historical documents which cannot be reasonably rejected, but must, on the contrary, be accepted by any normally intelligent, unbiased person as containing a faithful record of genuine historical events. I have proved from those records that Christ is truly God and that He founded a Church, the Catholic Church, which has come down through the ages quite unchanged and will remain unchanged until the end of the world. From the evidence I have so far submitted, you can easily, with God's help, now accept or assent to all the doctrines officially taught by the Catholic Church, as the teaching of Jesus Christ—as God's Revelation to man. However, I shall deal with those doctrines in detail, thus making it easier still for you to accept them. And, first of all, I shall treat of the Papacy, which enters into the very constitution of the Church as founded by Christ, and should therefore be dealt with before treating in detail of the other doctrines of the Church.

THE CHURCH MUST HAVE A HEAD

Every living thing—at least every living organism that is not merely rudimentary—has a head. You could not imagine a living fish or bird or animal not having a head, and you certainly could not imagine a living human being without a head. Likewise, every society, even an imperfect society, has a head. A football team must have a captain; a business firm must have a manager; and a city has its mayor. There is a head of every state or nation. A headless state or republic or kingdom is unthinkable.

Now, the Church is essentially a **society**. I had better explain this term briefly. A society is not a mere crowd or gathering of people. People are required to make a society, but a mere crowd or number of persons does not constitute a society. Something else is manifestly required. If, for instance, twenty persons just happened to be waiting together —having come from different places—to catch a train (or a car,) you would not call that group a society. Nor would you term all the people gathered together in a picture theatre a society. But, if twenty people formed a club, drew up rules, elected a president or chairman, a secretary, and a treasurer, you would have a little society—an imperfect society. Thus a tennis club or a football team may be termed a society. A society consists of human beings who band together for a definite aim or work or project; who act in unison or harmony, each doing his or her respective part; who have a definite code of rules; and who are guided by certain office-bearers under a chief leader That simple explanation will suffice.

The two perfect societies in the world are the Church and the State. The latter is a **natural** society, which cares for the temporal welfare or good of its citizens, while the former is a **supernatural** society, which leads its members to their eternal goal—the possession of God in the next life. In due time I shall explain to you the supernatural life. "One thing at a time" is a good rule, and I cannot expect you to absorb all Catholic teaching at once.

But, my dear friend, one thing should be evident to you at this stage as regards the constitution of the Church. **Since it is a society, it must have a head.** Can we suppose that the perfect supernatural society or kingdom instituted by the God-Man is alone, of all rightly constituted societies, without a head? Such a supposition would be a slur on the wisdom, power, and goodness of the Divine Founder of the Church. Reason revolts against such a supposition, reverence forbids it, faith repudiates it, revelation rejects it, history denies it.

WHO IS THE HEAD OF THE CHURCH?

Christ, of course, is the Supreme Head of the Church which He founded. But, since He was not to live in our midst, in His visible presence, He appointed a **visible head** of His Church—one who would rule as His vicegerent or vicar. Just as the Apostles and their successors were appointed to teach in the name of Christ ("He that heareth you heareth Me"), so one of the Apostles was appointed by Christ to rule the entire Church in His name and to have a lawful successor in that office till the end of time.

When we read the New Testament attentively, we see that Christ appointed Peter to this exalted office. And the history of early times clearly shows that the Bishop of Rome is Peter's lawful successor in that office of headship of Christ's Church.

Let me now, my dear inquirer, prove these statements. For the sake of greater clearness I shall set forth in three statements what I am going to prove to you in this and subsequent chats about the Papacy or Roman Primacy or Headship of Christ's Church:

1. Christ immediately and directly promised and

gave Peter the primacy of jurisdiction over the entire Church; that is, the supreme authority to rule the Church in His name.

2. Our Savior willed that this primary or supreme authority should continue in the Church until the end of the world.

3. The successors of Peter in this primacy are the Bishops of Rome.

1.—THE PRIMACY OF PETER

I could bring forward many texts from the New Testament to show that the primacy was conferred on Peter. But once more I remind you, my dear friend, that I am but giving you a rather summary course of Catholic doctrine, though I daresay that to you it seems very exhaustive. If you wish to study a more detailed treatment and proof of the Roman Primacy, you may take this booklet, "Who is the Pope?" which the Paulist Press of New York has published for me. (The remaining copies of the English edition, published by Sands and Company, have all been destroyed, with those of another work I had published, in the recent air raids on London.)

I shall single out the three most striking passages in the Gospels which show clearly that Peter was appointed chief or supreme ruler of the Church. I may mention that the original name of this Apostle was **Simon,** and that Christ, as we shall see, changed it into **Peter.** We find SS. Matthew and John calling him **Simon Peter.** Let us now consider the three passages to which I have referred.

"Jesus saith to them: But who do you say that I am? Simon Peter answered and said: Thou art Christ, the Son of the Living God.

"And Jesus, answering, said to him: Blessed art thou

Simon Bar-Jona, because flesh and blood hath not revealed it to thee, but My Father Who is in heaven.

"And I say to thee that thou art Peter, and upon this rock I will build My Church, and the gates of hell shall not prevail against it.

"And I will give to thee the keys of the kingdom of heaven. And whatsoever thou shalt bind on earth, it shall be bound also in heaven; and whatsoever thou shalt loose on earth, it shall be loosed also in heaven" (Matt. 16:15-19).

Five things strike our attention in this passage:

(a) Christ changes Simon's name to Peter or **rock**.

(b) Our Lord Himself promises to build His Church on this rock; that is, on Peter himself.

(c) He promises to establish His Church so firmly on this rock that the gates of hell shall never vanquish it.

(d) He promises to give Peter the keys of the Kingdom of Heaven.

(e) He promises him the power of binding and loosing.

METAPHOR OF THE ROCK

The English translation does not give us the full force of the original. Without taking you, my dear friend, into the intricacies of biblical language, you are aware that Christ did not speak in English, and that our English Bible is but a translation. The language which Christ used in the passage I have cited is known as **Aramaic**. In the English translation we have two distinct words, **Peter** and **rock**, although they have the same meaning. In Latin we have two almost identical words, **Petrus** and **petra**, which also have the very same meaning. In Greek the same occurs—**Petros** and **petra**. But the Greek and Latin versions of Matthew's

51

Gospel are but translations of the original Aramaic, written by the Evangelist himself. Now, in the Aramaic there are not two words, as in the versions I have quoted. Only one word, **kepha**, is used, and this word means rock. So that the really literal translation of Christ's words would be: "I say to thee that thou art a rock, and upon this rock I will build My Church."

You may rightly ask, then, why we find two words in the Latin, Greek, and English translations. The reason is simply that **petra** (rock) in Greek and Latin is a **feminine** noun, and it would be queer to give a man a feminine appellation; therefore a **masculine termination** was given, and the Apostle was called **Petros, Petrus.** It is for precisely the same reason that we call a boy **Patrick** and a girl **Patricia**, or a boy **Joseph** and a girl **Josephine.** The French version is a most accurate translation of the Aramaic, for it has the word **pierre** for both Peter and rock. **Pierre** is the French for **rock**, and it is also the name given to a boy as the equivalent of **Peter.**

You may wonder, my dear friend, why I have elaborated this point. Well, Protestants used formerly to make capital of the fact that in the English Bible (as if Christ had spoken in English!) two distinct words were used, and on this fact they strove to build a false argument by maintaining that the word **rock** did not refer to **Peter.** Nowadays, however, the more learned Protestants readily admit that the two words refer to the Apostle Simon or Peter. Thus Dr. Marsh, Anglican Bishop of Peterborough, wrote: "It seems a desperate undertaking to prove that Our Savior alluded to any other person than to St. Peter, for **the words of the passage can indicate no one else.**" ("Comparative View," Appendix Note D.)

We should notice, too, that the demonstrative adjective **this** in the phrase, "upon this rock," compels us grammatically to identify rock with Peter; otherwise the phrase would be meaningless.

Christ, then, promised **to build His Church on Peter.** Now, as the foundation of a building gives strength, stability, unity, and permanence to the building which is erected on it, so Peter must impart these qualities to the spiritual edifice known as the Church, and this he cannot do unless he exercises supreme authority (of teaching and ruling), over the entire Church. The Church is a society, and to say that Peter is the foundation of that society is to express in another form that he holds supreme authority over all its members, thus imparting to that society its stability and unity.

In our next chat I shall continue to develop the passage I have quoted from the sixteenth chapter of St. Matthew's Gospel, and shall then deal with two other Gospel passages which I shall quote for you.

CHAPTER IX.

THE PAPACY (Continued)

IN the remarkable promise made by Christ to Simon Peter and recorded in the sixteenth chapter of the Gospel of St. Matthew, the supreme authority Peter was to exercise over the Church is expressed in three metaphors. We have already considered the first; let us now pass on to the second.

THE METAPHOR OF THE KEYS

The second figure of speech is expressed in these words: "I will give to thee the keys of the kingdom of heaven." These words simply mean: "I will give thee supreme authority over my church." For (i) the **kingdom of heaven** here means the Church; and (ii) to be given the keys of a kingdom signifies to be appointed ruler of that kingdom.

(i) Christ often calls His Church "the kingdom of heaven." This is evident from the 13th chapter of St. Matthew, where the kingdom of heaven is compared to "a net cast into the sea, ·and **gathering together all kinds of fishes**" (both good and bad, as 48th verse tells us); and the 25th chapter, in which the kingdom of heaven is likened to ten virgins, five of whom were foolish and five wise. Since only the just may enter the kingdom of God's glory and of man's eternal happiness, usually termed **heaven** (about which we shall have a chat later), it is clear that the kingdom of heaven mentioned in these parables must refer to

54

Christ's kingdom on earth, that is, the Church, which embraces sinners as well as just.

(ii) The metaphor of the keys denotes supreme authority. Amongst various nations, especially in the Orient (where Christ spoke these words), keys have been regarded as a symbol of authority, and the sacred writers employ such symbolism, as may be seen from both the Old and the New Testament. You may, if you desire, verify this by turning to Isaias, XXII., 20-22, and Apocalypse, I., 18; v. 7, though I shall not ask you to take this trouble as you have not yet been introduced to the Old Testament.

THE METAPHOR OF BINDING AND LOSING

A third metaphor Christ used to express the supreme authority He was going to confer on Peter: "Whatsoever thou shalt bind on earth, it shall be bound also in heaven; and whatsoever thou shalt loose on earth, it shall be loosed also in heaven." Peter is here promised the power to bind his subjects, the members, that is, of Christ's Church, by laws, commands, censures, etc., and to free their souls from spiritual fetters—sins, punishment due to sins, ecclesiastical censures. In other words, Christ here promises to make Peter the sovereign ruler, the supreme legislator, in His kingdom, which is the Church.

Although this power of binding and loosing was later promised to the college of the Apostles (Matt. XVIII., 18), still it was promised first to Peter individually, to show that he was to possess it in a singular or eminent degree. To Peter alone, however, were two great prerogatives promised by his Divine Master: Peter individually was to be the rock-built foundation of Christ's Church, and Peter alone was to be the key-bearer of this kingdom—both of which metaphors, as I have shown, clearly contain the divine promise of jurisdiction or supreme authority over the entire Church.

CHRIST'S PRAYER FOR PETER

In His farewell words to the Apostles Our Savior declared: "I dispose to you, as my Father hath disposed to me, a kingdom." He then warned them, through Simon Peter, that Satan was plotting against that kingdom, striving to overthrow it at its inception by destroying the faith of the Apostles. "And the Lord said: Simon, Simon, behold Satan hath desired to have **you** (plural), that he may sift **you** (plural) as wheat" (Luke XXII., 31).

Note the plural in this text: Satan (about whom you will be told in due time—in a later chat) desired to have **all the Apostles.** Yet, wonderful to say, Christ prayed for **Peter individually** and appointed him to the office of **confirming his brethren** (the other Apostles), or keeping them in the faith. "But I have prayed for **thee,** that **thy** faith fail thee not, and thou being once converted **confirm thy brethren**" (ibid., v. 32).

Here we see Peter appointed to, or singled out **for,** the office of supreme teacher in Christ's kingdom, **the** Church.

THE BESTOWAL OF THE PRIMACY ON PETER

After His resurrection the Savior fulfilled, in unmistakable language, the solemn promise recorded by St. Matthew. The fulfilment of this promise is narrated in the twenty-first chapter of St. John's Gospel. Let us read together carefully verses 15-17.

Without taking you far into the realm of biblical language, I may state that St. John wrote his Gospel in Greek. The three English texts we have just read, "Feed my lambs . . . Feed my sheep," are slightly different in the original Greek, for the word lambs (in its equivalent Greek) occurs but once, while the Greek for **sheep** occurs twice. However, this slight variation in our English translation is unimportant, for both the Greek and the English show most clearly that Christ committed to Peter **His entire flock**—both lambs and sheep.

But the English word **feed** does not convey the full force of the original. In verse 15 it corresponds to the Greek; but in the following two cases (vv. 16 and 17) the Greek word employed really means **be shepherd over.** I may remark that the Greek word used invariably means, both in the Old and New Testament, to rule with authority, and that even pagan classical writers have used its equivalent noun, **shepherd or pastor,** as synonymous with **king** or **ruler.**

To sum up: Christ's words here mean, "Be shepherd over, or rule, my whole flock."

PETER EXERCISED SUPREME AUTHORITY

The Acts of the Apostles is a book written by Luke the Evangelist (although the authorship does not matter for the moment), giving an account of the Apostolic Church. You may read through this book at your leisure. But I would draw your attention just now to the fact that, although the author of this work is giving us, in the first twelve chapters, a short, general history of the Church, Peter's name is mentioned more than fifty times—more frequently than the names of all the other Apostles together. And consider the following striking facts: Peter proposes the choice of an Apostle in place of Judas; when Peter's name is mentioned with the names of the other Apostles, his name is always put first; Peter works the first miracle; Peter speaks to Annas, Caiphas, and others in the name of all the Apostles; Peter is the first to preach to the multitude; Peter judges Ananias and Saphira; Peter is the first to receive Gentiles into the Church;

Peter visits all the newly-established Christian communities; Peter's discourses are given at length.

Once more, my dear inquirer, I would remind you that in these "chats" I am striving to avoid a too elaborate explanation and also a too meagre exposition and proof of Catholic doctrine. Already I have more than once offered you books which deal in greater detail with the subjects about which we have been chatting. And, as regards Peter's office, I would recommend, for a fuller study of this matter, an admirable work written by a distinguished convert from the Anglican communion, "St. Peter, His Name, His Office, and His See," by T. W. Allies. Incidentally, I may mention that this work bears an excellent preface written by another prominent convert from Anglicanism, Rev. Luke Rivington, M.A., whose conversion was due, in great part, to a careful study of Peter's Primacy.

THE PRIMACY MUST LAST AS LONG AS THE CHURCH

Since the Church, according to the promises and institution of Christ, must last to the end of time, it necessarily follows that whatever is essential to it, in doctrine, in worship, in power, and in organization, must likewise perpetually endure.

The supreme Authority of which I have been speaking is surely essential to the Church. This is clear from the fact that Peter was appointed or constituted the **foundation** of the Church, the **key-bearer** of the kingdom, the **supreme teacher** (confirmer of his brethren in the faith), and the **sovereign shepherd** of the flock of Christ. Certainly a foundation is destined to last as long as the edifice raised on it; a key-bearer or chief ruler must hold office as long as a kingdom stands; a supreme teacher is required as long as there are brethren to be taught and kept in the unity of the faith; a chief shepherd is needed as long as there is a flock to be tended. Hence it is clear that the supreme office conferred on Peter must endure as long as the Church lasts, that is until the end of the world.

In our next chat I shall prove that the Roman Pontiff (the Bishop of Rome), whom we call the Pope, has lawfully inherited this supreme office in the Church of God.

CHAPTER X.

THE PAPACY (Continued)

S O far I have proved that the Divine Founder of the Church promised and gave Peter the primacy of jurisdiction (or supreme authority) over the entire Church, and that He willed this primacy to continue as long as the Church itself, that is, until the end of the world.

Let me now deal with the interesting question: Who, amongst all Bishops of the Universal Church, is Peter's successor in the primacy conferred on him by Christ? Our answer, given in the full light of genuine history, is very easy—**the Bishop of Rome.** Again we say with Cardinal Newman: "To be deep in history is to cease to be a Protestant."

Educated Protestants of to-day readily admit that St. Peter was in Rome, and even Bishop of that city. I shall not burden you, my dear friend, with the over-whelming evidence that Peter finally fixed his See in Rome and was martyred there during the fierce per-secution that broke out against the Christians under the despotic Emperor Nero. Before, however, pro-ceeding further, I shall quote two Protestant writers.

The Rev. Dr. Robertson wrote: "It is not so much a spirit of sound criticism as a religious prejudice which has led some Protestants to deny that the Apostle (Peter) was ever at Rome, where all ancient testimony represents him to have suffered, together with St. Paul, in the reign of Nero." And Bishop Ellicot declared, "Nothing but Protestant prejudice can stand against the historical evidence that St. Peter sojourned and died in Rome."

In the present chat, my dear searcher after truth, I shall show that the Bishops of Rome have ever claimed, as successors of St. Peter, supreme authority over the Church, and that this claim has been constantly recognized by the Church.

THE ROMAN PONTIFFS HAVE EVER CLAIMED AND EXERCISED SUPREME AUTHORITY

1. The most ancient Christian document after the writings of the Apostles is the letter of Clement to the Corinthians. St. Clement was the third successor of St. Peter as Bishop of Rome. The order of the first four Popes is this: Peter, Linus, Cletus, Clement. St. John the Apostle and Evangelist was still living during the reign of Clement. About the year 95 a dissension arose at Corinth. Yet it was **Clement, not John,** who authoritatively intervened, for Clement, as Peter's successor, was the Head of the Church. Here are a few passages from Clement's letter (you will see how he spoke with authority—with the authority of a ruler—even to the Christians in what was then distant Corinth):

"It will be no light sin in us to deprive of the episcopate those who offer the gifts blamelessly and holily. . . . If certain persons should be disobedient to the words spoken by Him (God) through us, let them understand that they will entangle themselves in no slight transgression and danger, but we shall be guiltless of the sin. . . . Learn to be subject, laying aside all proud and arrogant boasting of your tongues; for it is better for you to be found little and approved

61

in the sheepfold of Christ than to seem to yourselves better than others and be cast out of the fold."

2. **Victor** was Bishop of Rome during the last decade of the second century. He threatened to cut off from the Church those Asiatic Bishops who would not conform to the Western custom regarding the celebration of Easter. The great St. Irenaeus, of whom I have already spoken in these chats, did not question the Pope's authority to excommunicate Asiatic Bishops, but simply pleaded with Victor not to carry out his threat.

3. When the brilliant scholar and eminent churchman, **Athanasius, Patriarch of Alexandria,** had been unjustly accused and deposed by his enemies, he appealed to Pope Julius (337-352). The Pope heard the case and pronounced Athanasius innocent. Consider this extract from the letter of Julius and you will see that he claimed the very same authority as the Pope to-day:

"He (Athanasius) came (to Rome) not of himself, but **cited by us.** . . . Know you not that this was the custom, that we should have been written to first, and that the right judgment should go forth from this place. . . . For what we have received from the Apostle Peter, this I also declare to you."

CLEAR TESTIMONY OF THE EARLY FATHERS

Those great scholars and writers (many of whom were Bishops) of the early ages of Christianity are called the Fathers of the Church. Coming so soon after the Apostles, from whom they had received the rich legacy of Christ's revelation, their testimony is of great weight. Let us see what they have to say about the supremacy of the Bishop of Rome. I shall single out but a few testimonies:

1. Writing of the Roman Church (i.e., the Church established in the City of Rome), St. Irenaeus says: "For it is necessary that every church, that is, those (faithful) who are everywhere, agree with this church because of its greater authority, in which (church) the tradition which is from the Apostles has been preserved by those who are everywhere."

2. St. Cyprian, Bishop of Carthage, who was martyred in the year 258, teaches that "there is one Church, founded by the Lord on Peter for the origin and purpose of unity." He calls the Church at Rome "the root and womb of the Catholic Church," and complains that the followers of the pseudo-bishop, Fortunatus, "dare sail to the Chair of Peter and to the chief Church, from which priestly union has arisen." And again he asks: "Does he who opposes and resists the Church, and who deserts the Chair of Peter, upon which the Church was founded, trust that he is in the Church?"

3. St. Jerome was the greatest scriptural scholar of the early ages. He lived from 340 to 420, and because of his scholarship was held in the highest esteem throughout the Church. Yet, in regard to the Roman Pontiff, he shows the submissiveness and docility of a child. Here is a letter written by him from the East to Pope Damasus:

"Although your greatness makes me afraid, still your kindness invites. From the priest I entreat safety for the victim, from the shepherd protection for the sheep. Let the glory of the Roman summit withdraw; I am speaking with the successor of the fisherman and the disciple of the cross. Following no chief but Christ, I am united in communion with your Blessedness, that is, with the Chair of Peter. Upon that rock I know that the Church is built. Whoever eats the lamb outside this house is unholy. . . . Therefore I entreat your Blessedness through the crucified Savior of the world, through the consubstantial Trinity, to give me authority by your letters either to abstain from or to declare the hypostases." This letter referred to a point of doctrine, which the great Jerome asked the Roman Pontiff, as the Supreme Shepherd of the flock, to decide authoritatively, promising to accept wholeheartedly the Pope's decision.

Three rival Bishops claimed the See of Antioch. How was Jerome to find out who was the lawful Bishop? He passed over the Patriarchs of Jerusalem, Alexandria, and Constantinople, who were nearer to him, and sought guidance from distant Rome. Consider this extract from a second letter to Pope Damasus:

"Here the Church, torn into three factions, hastens to snatch me to itself. . . . Meanwhile I continue to call out: 'If anyone is united to the Chair of Peter, he is mine.' Meletius, Vitalis, and Paulinus say that they adhere to you. I could believe if one said this: Now either two or all are lying. Therefore I implore your Blessedness . . . to signify by your letters with whom I should be in union in Syria."

ɔ 4. As Jerome was the brilliant scholar in Scripture, Augustine, Bishop of Hippo, was the outstanding scholar of that time, and of all time, in theology. Yet he, too, harkened with childlike docility to the authoritative teaching of the Bishop of Rome, the Supreme Teacher of the Church of God. Two councils (meetings of Bishops) were held in Africa to deal with the errors of the Pelagians. (What those errors were you need not at present inquire—you cannot, my dear friend, absorb all doctrine at once). The decrees of the councils were sent to Rome, to be submitted to the Pope. This is what the great Augustine wrote when the answer came from Rome:

"Concerning this cause (Pelagianism) the decrees of two councils have already been sent to the Apostolic See; thence the rescripts have come. **The cause is finished.**" This statement of Augustine has been crystallised into the well-known saying, "Rome has spoken; the cause is finished."

GENERAL COUNCILS AND THE ROMAN PRIMACY

An Ecumenical or General Council is a formal meeting of all the Bishops of the Church, assembled to define matters of faith and morals or to legislate for the Universal Church. The manner in which General Councils have been, from the earliest times, convoked, conducted, and terminated clearly shows that the Bishop of Rome is the Head of the Church, as successor of St. Peter. I shall draw your attention to a few features of a few Councils; this will be sufficient, for I must not give you a long lecture on Church history:

1. The **Council of Nice** (or Nicaea), a town in Bithynia, was held in the year 325, during the reign of Pope Sylvester. Over this historic assembly of Bishops, most of whom were from the East, **three Papal legates presided,** and the formulary of faith adopted was drawn up by one of them, Hosius, a Spaniard.

2. The **Council of Ephesus** was held in 431, during the pontificate of Celestine, who was represented by three legates, two Bishops and a priest, as well as by Cyril of Alexandria. In the third session, Philip, though only a priest (one of the Papal legates), spoke thus to the assembled Bishops:

"It is doubtful to none, yea, rather has it been known to all ages, that the most holy and most blessed Peter, the Prince and Head of the Apostles, the pillar of faith, received from our Lord Jesus Christ the keys of the kingdom, and to him was given power to bind and loose; **who, even until now, and always, both lives and exercises judgment in his successors.** Wherefore, our most blessed Pope, Celestine, Bishop, his successor in order and holder of his place, has sent us to the Holy Synod as representative of his person. As, therefore, Nestorius, the author of this new impiety, has not only allowed the term **fixed by the Apostolic See** to pass by, but also a much longer period of time, the sentence on him stands ratified by a decree of all the churches. . . . Wherefore let Nestorius know that he is cut off from communion with the priesthood of the Catholic Church."

3. The **Council of Chalcedon** was held in 451, during the reign of Pope Leo the Great, who sent four legates, two bishops and two priests, to whom he gave very definite instructions. These are the Pope's words to that celebrated Council which, be it noted, was held in the East (Chalcedon was opposite Constantinople, on the Bosphorus):

"Let your fraternity consider that in these brethren who have been directed by the Apostolic See I myself preside over the Council. . . Therefore, dearest brethren, reject altogether boldness of disputing, and let the vain unbelief cease of those who err; and let it not be allowed to defend what it is not lawful to believe."

Some six hundred Bishops took part in the Council. Although the vast majority of them hailed from the East, they harkened with the docility of children to the voice of the Bishop of Rome conveyed to them through his legates. In the second session the dogmatic letter of Pope Leo was read. On hearing it, the large gathering of Bishops exclaimed with **one voice** and one heart: "This is the faith of Peter; this is **the** faith of the Apostles. . . **Peter has spoken through Leo."**

CHAPTER XI.

THE SOURCES OF REVELATION

NOTE: At this stage of the chats or instructions, or even earlier, many an inquirer will have arrived at the conviction that the Catholic Church is the infallible exponent of revealed truth, and will be ready, by the grace of faith, to assent firmly to whatever the Church teaches as revealed by God and also to accept wholeheartedly whatever else she officially teaches (for the moment this last sentence need not be amplified). At any rate, the writer's experience has been that many inquirers, who at the beginning had no intention of embracing the Catholic faith, have gladly made their submission after a few chats.

From now on, in these chats, I shall treat our inquirer as a prospective convert, who has clearly expressed his intention of entering the Fold of Peter. Of course, as I deal with individual doctrines, I shall continue to offer suitable proofs of them.

THE FOUNTAINS OF REVEALED TRUTH

You have now, my dear friend, definitely accepted the Catholic position, and I heartily congratulate you. You readily admit and assent to the truth that there is a God, the infinite Being. You are convinced that He has graciously given a revelation to mankind, the fulness of that revelation having been given by Jesus Christ, God Incarnate. You firmly hold that the Catholic Church is divine and that she is the infallible exponent or teacher of God's revealed truth. And you are quite ready to assent explicitly or expressly to each doctrine which she officially teaches, and which you have now already accepted at least implicitly. You have, my dear friend, arrived at this blessed state of mind by the aid of God's grace, about which you will be told in due time. In a word, you have now, by God's grace, made your **Act of Faith.** You are now desirous of learning the individual doctrines of the Church with a view to being received into the Church. Thus you are what is termed a **catechumen**—one who is at heart a Catholic and is being prepared for formal reception into the Church.

While setting before you the official teaching of the Church and explaining each doctrine, I shall at the same time give you suitable proofs of these doctrines, so that you may grasp them more easily and be able to give a reason of the faith that is in you. But, before descending to particulars, I wish to tell you about the Fountains of Revealed Truth—those wells or springs whence the Church draws forth for us her divine doctrines, and which are aptly termed the **Sources of Revelation** (or Revealed Truth). Having done this, I shall then show you the great difference, the essential difference, between the Catholic religion and Protestantism—the **fundamental** difference between the two. I shall show you, that is, the fundamental difference between the Catholic and Protestant **Rule of Faith**—the important, underlying principle which guides us in determining what doctrines exactly we must believe.

In order to explain to you the source—or, rather, the twin sources—of God's revealed truth, I shall first offer you an easy illustration.

A SIMPLE EXAMPLE

Imagine two lovely tanks or wells, connected by a pipe which will allow the water to pass from one to the other. Then picture a great shower of rain falling from the clouds and filling both tanks. See a number of thirsty children standing near those tanks or wells while their mother draws pure, crystal, refreshing water for each child.

Well, you may ask, what has that to do with our chat? It is an example, my dear convert, that will be helpful to you. The thirsty children represent human souls (the members of the human race in this life), the mother represents the Church, the heavenly shower signifies Divine Revelation, and the two tanks or wells stand for the twin source in which are contained the truths of revelation. These two sources are called **Scripture** and **Tradition.**

MEANING OF SACRED SCRIPTURE AND DIVINE TRADITION

The Sacred Scriptures comprise the books of the Old and the New Testament. I have already proved to you that the New Testament is a collection of genuine, truthful, historical documents. But the infallible Church teaches that they are also **inspired,** that is, that they were written by Apostles (or disciples of Apostles) under the direct influence of God, Who moved the sacred writers to write what they did and guided them in the actual writing so as to exclude all possible error. The Church teaches likewise that the Old Testament is inspired. You will have time enough to learn more about the Old Testament later on. Thus whatever is found in the Bible is God's Own Truth. But the Bible is not the only (or complete) fountain or source of revealed truth, for only a few of the

Apostles were inspired to write Gospels or Epistles, and even these few did not profess to write a full record of Christ's teaching, as we shall see in our next chat.

Whatever revealed truths were not written down under divine inspiration, but were handed down by the Apostles by word of mouth to their lawful successors (and have been constantly taught by the Church) are known as **Divine Tradition.** "Scripture" means "writing" or "something written"; "Tradition" means "handing down" or "something handed down."

Sometimes our non-Catholic friends ask us where a certain Catholic doctrine is found in the Bible. The answer is that Sacred Scripture does not contain all the water that fell from the heavens. Some of the truths which God has revealed are contained in Tradition, which is as pure and holy a spring or source as the Bible.

As the children mentioned could not, by themselves, get that refreshing water from the tanks or wells, but needed their mother's sure help, so men cannot safely or reliably get doctrines—at least all revealed doctrines—from the two sources I have mentioned (the Bible and Tradition) without the unfailing help, the infallible guidance, of the Church.

You must have noticed that I pictured the two tanks or wells as connected by a pipe, so that water may flow from one to the other. For years after Christ's ascension there was no written New Testament, and the doctrines of Christ were preached and taught by the Apostles by word of mouth. Only by degrees and after long years was the full New Testament completed in written form—I mean the books which make up what we call the New Testament. Some of the waters of revelation were gradually flowing from the well of Tradition into the well of Scripture, although all the water did not pass into the latter well.

Let me now, my dear catechumen, sum up this chat: **All the truths that God has revealed to His Church are contained in two sources, Scripture and Tradition, and only the Catholic Church can tell us, without the slightest error, what those truths are. We firmly believe all that God has revealed because God is Truth itself. And we know with the greatest certainty what God has revealed because the Church infallibly (without the slightest danger of error) tells us.**

CHAPTER XII.

CATHOLIC AND PROTESTANT RULE OF FAITH

THOSE Christians who reject the infallible authority of the Catholic Church offer a strange substitute. They say that the Bible is the complete record or only source of God's revelation to mankind and that it should be interpreted according to the private judgment of each individual. The Catholic Church, on the contrary, maintains that the Bible is but a partial depository of Divine Revelation (as I explained in our last chat), and that the inspired Book is to be interpreted not according to the private judgment of the individual, but by the living, infallible Church.

Thus Protestantism and Catholicism differ fundamentally on two matters—the source or fountain of Revelation, and the means of recognizing the truths contained in that source. In this chat, my dear catechumen, I shall prove that the Bible is not the complete record or only source of Revelation; in our next chat I shall deal with the question of Private Judgment.

THE BIBLE CANNOT PROVE ITS OWN INSPIRATION

We ask our non-Catholic friends this fair question: If you reject the authority of the Church, how can you know which book is the Bible?

Let us bear in mind that the Bible is not really a single book, but a collection of many books which were written at various times. Now, take any particular book in the Bible. How do you know that such a work is inspired? Obviously, unless you wish to contradict your own rule of faith, you must banish every authority or extrinsic agent and prove the inspiration of such work from within.

Do you hold that the book is inspired just because it says it is inspired? But this would be supposing the very thing to be proved, what we call begging the question (petitio principii)—supposing the inspiration of the very book whose inspiration you wish to prove. Besides, how many books of the Bible speak of their own inspiration? It would be surprising to you to find the answer to this question.

Is it the subject-matter of the book that convinces you that the work is inspired? This test also fails to work, for in the Bible we find (in certain books) accounts of revolting sins and atrocious crimes. God no doubt had His wise reasons for moving the human writer to record these things, but, from the nature of the matter, we should not infer that the record is inspired. And, if you apply the test of sublime matter, why do you, after granting that Genesis is inspired, reject the Book of Wisdom, which the Catholic Church teaches to be inspired? Why, after admitting as inspired the Song of Solemon (the Canticle of Canticles), do you reject the Book of Ecclesiasticus? These two books which Protestantism rejects are certainly more sublime and elevating than those two which it admits as inspired.

Our Protestant friend may say that he accepts as inspired those books of the Old Testament which Christ quoted, and those books of the New Testament which were written by Apostles. We reply: As regards the first part of your statement, we would remind you that you are appealing to an authority which is extrinsic to the book in question. Besides Christ gave comparatively few quotations from the Old Testament, and you can logically attribute inspiration only to these isolated quotations. As to the second part of your statment, we ask: Why, then, admit the inspiration of the Gospels of Mark and Luke, who were not Apostles?

You have a greater difficulty when we come to the question of the inspiration of the whole Bible. Certainly it required an extrinsic agent to recognize as inspired each book—to choose it from amongst so many other documents—and to collect all those various books from Genesis to the Apocalypse (the Book of Revelations). This is evident, for a number of inanimate documents, written at various times and places during the course of long centuries, could not fly spontaneously together into one volume, and exclaim triumphantly: "Look at me; I am the Bible!" An **extrinsic, living agent** must have recognized those documents or books and collected them into the present Bible. Do you, my dear Protestant friend, admit the **reliability** or rather **infallibility** of this agent? If not, then, alas! you can never be sure that your Bible is God's word. For us Catholics, of course, there is no difficulty; this agent is certainly infallible, for it is the Church of Christ, without which we could not determine which books are inspired.

THE BIBLE DOES NOT CLAIM TO CONTAIN ALL REVELATION

If the Bible alone is the source of Revelation; if we are not to believe as revealed by God anything not found in the Bible, then we should not believe this very truth (that the Bible contains all God's teaching), unless it is contained in the Bible. But in vain will our non-Catholic search the Scriptures for any such claim on the part of the Bible. In fact, quite the contrary is stated and, indeed, most emphatically. It is rather amusing to find that the most emphatic condemnation of the Bible alone theory is found in the Bible itself. Protestants, therefore, who profess to believe the Bible, should admit, on the Bible's own word, that the Bible is not the complete record, the only fount, of God's revealed truth.

I would ask our Protestant friends to consider the following stern facts:

1. During the three years' training of the Apostles Christ did not once tell them to write (if we take the written Gospel as the source of our information). Texts in abundance are found which show that their Divine Master commanded them to **teach and preach** but not a single text is found to show that He commanded them to write. Now, if Christ's revelation was to be contained only in the written Word, is it conceivable that He would have left them free not to write that Revelation? And is it likely that only two out of the twelve would have written Gospels, and then so long after their Master's ascension? Is it credible that only four of them would have written Epistles, some of which are exceedingly meagre?

If the Bible alone contains all God's revelation, then, strange to say, Christians could not have known for the first sixty years of the Church's existence what truths Christ had taught, for the Gospels were not completed until sixty years had passed.

2. St. John was the last Evangelist to write. Yet his closing words ran thus: "But there are also **many other things which Jesus did;** but if every one of these should be written, not even the world itself, I think, could hold the books that would have to be written."

3. The Epistles of St. Paul, which Protestants rightly accept as part of the inspired Bible, most clearly assert that the Scriptures alone do not contain all that we must believe. Consider, e.g., the following passages:—

"Therefore, brethren, stand fast, and hold the traditions which you have learned, whether by word or by our epistle" (2 Thess. II., 14).

"The things which thou hast heard of me by many witnesses, the same commend to faithful men, who shall be fit to teach others also" (2 Tim. II., 2).

"How shall they believe in Him of whom they have not heard? And how shall they hear without a preacher? . . . Therefore faith cometh by hearing, and hearing by the word of Christ" (Romans 10, 14-17).

IMPOSSIBLE FOR MANY TO GET OR READ THE BIBLE

Even had the Apostles written a complete exposition of the Christian religion (which, as I have shown, they had not the remotest intention of doing), how were they to disseminate or circulate their books? Printing was not invented as yet, and to transcribe the New Testament, not to speak of the entire Bible, would have taken a very considerable time, and consequently but few copies, comparatively speaking, would have been procurable. Besides, written works were very costly; what were those poor people to do who could not buy a Bible? Again, many persons were unable to read; was God's Revelation intended only for the learned? Then what of those numberless people who could read, but who could not understand Hebrew or Aramaic or Greek? Were they to look for a learned friend to translate into their own language the Scriptures? And, if they could find such a friend, what guarantee would they have had that he was giving them a true translation?

Surely our loving Redeemer, Who shed His blood for all men, never intended the precious graces of Redemption, which flow from His enlightening doctrine, to reach only the rich and the learned?

CHAPTER XIII.

PRIVATE JUDGMENT

IN our last chat, my dear convert, I showed you that the Bible does not contain the whole of God's revealed truth; that it is but a partial depository of Revelation; that it is only one of two equally pure fountains of Divine Teaching. In the present chat I am going to prove to you that the Bible should not be interpreted by what is called **private judgment,** or the sense or understanding of each individual. Let me first give you a simple example.

We shall suppose that a discussion arises about the meaning of a certain law of the land—some important enactment of the State. Now, just imagine what would happen if every citizen put his own interpretation on that statutory or legal document and acted accordingly! You may work this out for your own amusement regarding dozens of laws that you know. The principle is absurd. In every well regulated State there is a duly appointed supreme tribunal of competent jurists—a group of eminent judges—whose verdict determines the meaning of the laws of the State when controversies arise. I shall mention one such interesting case. When I arrived in America in 1923 (in November), a law had been passed in the State of Oregon, according to which law all children in that State would be obliged, from the age of eight (I think) to sixteen, to attend some **public school.** Thus, according to that law, all Catholic children would have been compelled to give up attending a Catholic school. The law was passed under the influence of the Ku Klux Klan (a crazy, bigoted, secret organization), whose pernicious influence dominated the members of both houses of the legislature in the State of Oregon and also evidently the Governor, who signed the Bill. But the Catholics knew the Constitution of the United States, and so they appealed to the Supreme Court, which, after duly hearing the case, declared the law **unconstitutional.** Every intelligent American then "had the laugh on" the wiseacres in the Oregon legislative houses and on the wonderful Governor of the State!

Sometimes—or, rather, more often—the supreme legal authority in a country has to decide, not the question as to whether a certain law is constitutional, but the meaning of certain clauses of the law.

Now, can we imagine that, while ordinary men, often pagans, have the sense to establish a competent authority for the correct interpretation of human laws, Christ would have failed in so vital a matter and left His written Law (the inspired Bible) to be understood and interpreted just as each member of the human race, or each individual Christian, thought fit? Such a supposition is evidently absurd and is also an insult to the wisdom of God Incarnate.

THE BIBLE A DIFFICULT BOOK TO INTERPRET

The very difficulty of such interpretation renders private judgment impracticable as a means of ascertaining the true meaning of the Scriptures. When we consider the various human authors (under God's inspiration) who have written, each in his own style, the books that constitute the Bible; when we consider the many figures of speech (generally oriental) they employ; when we realize the sublimity of the matter of which they frequently treat, and especially the vagueness and obscurity of the prophetic books—when we consider all this, we can easily see that private judgment is a futile principle.

PRIVATE JUDGMENT SELF-CONTRADICTORY

This means fails also for the reason that, in practice, it is self-contradictory. Just look at the number of conflicting sects that have sprung up from the application of the principle of private judgment, and consider the hopeless differences of opinion within the same sect, without any competent authority to decide which is right. Why, a few years ago Dr. Angus, a Presbyterian minister and professor in Sydney, publicly denied the **Divinity of Christ.** Vehement discussions ensued, but Dr. Angus still maintains his opinion—and his place of honor as a Presbyterian! In the Anglican Church we see Bishop Barnes, of Birmingham, England, teaching doctrines opposed to the very essence of Christianity, and yet going along "smiling and serene," continuing his work as bishop (save the mark!). I know from personal chats with fervent Anglicans how keenly they feel this, but they are powerless to do anything about it, just as the Presbyterians of Sydney are unable to do anything effective in the case of Dr. Angus. Once the principle of the Bible alone and private judgment is admitted, I fail to see what effectual steps they can take.

THE BIBLE ITSELF CONDEMNS PRIVATE JUDGMENT

The Scriptures themselves not only do not approve of the free exercise of private judgment, in matters of faith, but, on the contrary, emphatically condemn it.

Our Divine Lord threatens with everlasting condemnation those who will not believe the doctrines preached by the living, authoritative voice of the Apostles,
and He places on a level with the heathen and the
publican those who will not hear the Church. Evidently, then, private judgment, far from being the
prescribed means of interpreting Scripture, can even
lead souls to perdition.

The Bible expressly repudiates private judgment.
Thus St. Peter writes of St. Paul's Epistles: "As also
in his epistles, speaking in them of these things, in
which are certain things **hard to be understood, which
the unlearned and unstable wrest, as they do also the
other Scriptures, to their own destruction**" (2 Peter,
III., 16). The same Apostle tells us that "no prophecy
of Scripture is made by private interpretation" (ibid.
I., 20).

The need of an authoritative exponent of **the**
written word is shown by several striking examples.
The two disciples, journeying to Emmaus, although
they knew well the Scriptures, were quite at a loss to
understand them until Christ Himself explained them.
And, when Philip the deacon heard the Ethiopian reading the prophecy of Isaiah, he asked: "Thinkest thou
that thou understandest what thou readest?" To which
the eunuch replied: "And how can I, unless someone
show me!" Whereupon Philip explained to him the
mystery of Redemption, got him to make his act of
faith, and forthwith baptised him.

PRACTICE OF PROTESTANTS CONTRADICTS THEIR OWN THEORY

Since the Protestant Rule of Faith is really un-
workable, non-Catholics contradict in practice what
they formulate in theory. The Protestant child re-

ceives the Bible on a merely human authority—on the word of its parents or Sunday school teacher. The educated Protestant admits the inspiration of the Bible on the authority of Tradition, or, what may seem more remarkable still, on the authority of the Church of Rome "Deny the Scripture also," wrote Luther in sarcasm to Zwingli, "for **we have received it, too, from the Pope.**"

"I would not believe the Gospel," wrote the great luminary St. Augustine, eleven centuries before Luther, "unless the authority of the Church moved me to do so."

Nor do our non-Catholic friends embrace only those doctrines and laws taught in Scripture; otherwise they would keep holy the **Sabbath** (Saturday) and not **Sunday.** For us Catholics there is no difficulty in this matter, for, as I have already explained, the Bible is not the only depository of God's truth, and, besides, the Church has power to legislate. The observance of the Sabbath was, at least in part, a mere ceremonial law of the Jewish religion. Certainly the natural law prescribes that we should set apart some time for the worship of our Creator. In the Old Law God designated the seventh day of the week (the Sabbath) as the day of rest and prayer and prescribed in detail how it was to be spent. Protestants, who profess to follow the Bible alone, should return to that Jewish practice. The Catholic explanation is that this ceremonial law of the Jewish law ceased, like the Jewish sacrifices and circumcision, by the establishment of the New Testament by Jesus Christ. Then the Church, exercising her legislative power, commanded her members to observe, instead of the seventh day of the week, the first day, in honor of Christ's glorious Resurrection. She also determined, and still determines, in what way her members are to sanctify that day.

It is evident, too, that the Protestant privilege of private judgment is greatly circumscribed in practice. Why all this disturbance in a home (in so many cases) when a member of a Protestant family decides to become a Catholic? To those who object, surely the convert may reasonably answer: "You tell me that I must interpret the Bible by my own intelligence, or according to my own private judgment. Well, my dear family, that is just what I am doing. I have read the Gospels and the Epistles, and it is as clear as day to me that Christ founded a living, infallible Church, which could not change. That Church must be the Catholic Church. I have fully satisfied my private judgment on that important point. Now, in seeking admission into the Catholic Church, whose doctrines I shall then wholeheartedly accept by the gift of faith, I am but following my own interpretation of the Bible. Please allow me to exercise this grand privilege of private judgment and let us all live together affectionately and happily."

NOT A VICIOUS CIRCLE

A **vicious circle** is the name given to one example of **false** reasoning. It is committed if one proved A from **B, and** then B from A. Here is an example: "William is Samuel's father, because Samuel is William's son." I once heard a Bishop examining a number of children for Confirmation. The Bishop asked a certain boy: "How should we keep Sunday?" The boy at once answered: "As we keep holidays." "And how should we keep holidays?" asked his Lordship. To the evident amusement of the Bishop and parish priest, the lad answered promptly: "As we keep Sunday."

Now, some persons who think themselves smart sometimes object: "You Catholics argue in a vicious circle, for you prove the Church from the Bible and then the Bible from the Church."

The answer is simple. One method of proving the truth of the Catholic Church is the historical method, although it is not the only one. I have given it special (though not exclusive) attention in these chats. I would sum it up thus:

First we prove, by the accepted rules of historical criticism, that, as **ordinary human documents,** as ordinary **historical records,** the four Gospels are genuine, intact, and truthful. The **inspiration** of the Scriptures does not enter into this matter at all.

We next prove, as I have done in these chats, from the reliable historical documents mentioned, that Christ established a living, infallible Church. And on the authority of this Church we accept by faith whatever she proposes to our belief. One of the articles she teaches is that the Bible is inspired. This we assent to as an article of Divine and Catholic faith, a truth revealed by God to His Church and declared to us as such by her infallible authority.

You have now, my dear catechumen, traversed the whole field of general or fundamental defence of the Church's position in this world. It remains for me to talk over with you her individual doctrines.

CHAPTER XIV.

THE CREATION OF MAN

OUR reason tells us that God alone is eternal, self-existent, infinite, and that all else was made by Him. In this chat I shall talk of the visible world—that world of things that come under our senses. This includes men, although the chief element in man—his soul—is a spirit, that is, something that can exist and act independently of matter. But in this life the human soul is united to the body to form a complete human nature. However, my dear catechumen, we shall come to the soul presently.

The world was **created** by God. To create means to produce or make out of nothing. When we make a thing, e.g., a bench or a bicycle or a house, we always require some previous or already existing material to work with. But God, since He is all-powerful, can create. He **created** the first material elements and **fashioned** the world in its present form from them. And we shall see presently that He created the first human soul, as He continues to create every human soul.

THE BIBLE AND CREATION

Here is a complete Bible. You may take it with you if you wish, though I certainly do not ask you to read it through just now or in the near future. In fact, I do not ask you to read it through at all. But it will be well to have it at least for reference. In this chat I shall go over the first chapter, which begins: "In the beginning God created heaven and earth."

Although the writer of the chapter (as the writers of every portion of the Bible) was inspired, we must remember that it was not his intention to write what we call a **scientific treatise** on astronomy or geology or biology or natural history. It has been well said that "the Bible tells us how to go to heaven, and not how the heavens go." The first chapter of Genesis (that is the name of the first book in the Bible) is a wonderful account of the origin of things. But it was written for a simple people, and the inspired author (Moses) adapted his account to the capacity of that people. He had no intention of giving a recital of the scientific order, even if he knew this, which is not likely. Nor had he any intention of giving us a strictly chronological order—an account of events in the exact order in which they proceeded.

His real aim was to teach us that God created the world and especially man. The account he gives us **is historical** and **popular;** this means that it is a narrative of actual events or true occurrences, but given in a form that any ordinary chronicler or historian chooses to suit his readers.

EXAMPLE OF HISTORICAL AND POPULAR NARRATIVE

Let us suppose that an American writer decided to produce a life of Theodore Roosevelt. He would naturally divide the work into chapters. But, chronologically, these chapters would **overlap.** What I mean is that certain events mentioned in the first chapter might have occurred after other events mentioned in the second chapter, and so on. The author might consider Mr. Roosevelt's life as a student or reader, as a politician, as a sportsman, as a friend, as a man interested in works of charity, etc. Suppose that the writer divided the life into seven chapters. It can be seen quite easily that, although all the events recorded in the book do not follow in strict chronological order, still the work is historical. In a word, it would be "historical and popular."

Now, the inspired writer very probably **grouped,** for the sake of an easy narrative, the works of creation. Thus he used the word **day,** not to express a period of twenty-four hours, but to facilitate the order of the historical narrative—the account of actual events. In this way he grouped day and night (first day); sea and sky, or sea and atmosphere, including clouds (second day); land under water, or sea, and land over water, or continents and islands (third day); sun and moon and stars (fourth day); fish, reptiles, and birds (fifth day); animals and man (sixth day).

Such an interpretation, which is quite reasonable, can never conflict with the genuine discoveries of science, which the Church heartily welcomes. As I have already pointed out, my dear convert, the inspired writer had no intention of writing a work on science. But I would stress the fact, in passing, that there can never be any real conflict between the official teaching of the Church and the discoveries and genuine conclusions of true science, for God, who is Infinite Truth, is the author of both Nature and Revelation, and Truth cannot contradict itself.

Some Catholic writers understand the word **day** in Genesis as an **indefinite period,** extending over even thousands of years. And, indeed, it is remarkable how the general order of creation given in the Book of Genesis corresponds with that outlined by great scientists who have studied the development of the universe and this earth of ours.

If you wish to go deeper into these questions, I shall lend you suitable books, especially "The Church and Science," by a distinguished scholar in science and a great convert to the Catholic Faith, Sir Bertram Windle. But the summary I have given you is sufficient for our present purpose.

CREATION OF MAN

The noblest creature in the visible universe is man. He is essentially superior to the brute creation, for he has a spiritual, immortal soul, which is the principle of all his life. Our reason tells us that we have such a soul. Man can think, judge, and reason. He has a free-will. He has a moral sense or conscience. He has articulate speech, whereby he can communicate his ideas and knowledge to his fellow-men. These attributes can belong only to a spiritual principle (such as a rational soul), which renders man essentially superior to irrational animals. He is, in a sense, the lord of the world, subject, of course, to his Creator. God's revelation also teaches us that we have a soul, that it is endowed with freedom, and that it is immortal. The Bible tells us, therefore, that God made or created man "to His own image and likeness." Man is the image of God especially in his spiritual, intelligent (or, rather, rational), free soul; and he is the likeness of God especially in the supernatural life with which God gifted our first parents, Adam and Eve. I must explain this expression.

SUPERNATURAL LIFE

The word supernatural means above nature. Reason, free-will, and the moral law are natural to man. But God elevated (lifted up) man from the beginning to a life far higher and nobler than the natural life

—to the supernatural life. He gave our first parents a wondrous gift known as **grace,** whereby they partook in a mysterious manner of God's Own life; He endowed them with faith and hope and charity Of these gifts you will learn more later on. And God gave them also freedom from death, suffering, ignorance, and the lust of the flesh. He intended that all these wonderful gifts should pass to Adam's descendants. How Adam lost them both for himself and for us, though he kept his natural gifts, I shall explain in our next chat, in which I shall tell you about original Sin.

NOTE: In this chat, in speaking of the creation of man, I have not treated the question of evolution **(1)** because the average convert is not greatly concerned with this matter and is quite prepared, when he has reached the present stage of the chats, to accept wholeheartedly the teaching of the Church, and **(2)** because I wish to keep these chats within a reasonable limit. The instructor may, however, briefly explain that, although God directly or immediately created the soul of Adam and also immediately creates every human soul, He did not immediately create the body of Adam, but **formed** it from the earth, as the second chapter of Genesis, verse 7, tells us. It is the traditional teaching of the Church that God directly formed this body from the earth, although it is not against any official teaching to hold that the body of the first man was evolved from a higher animal. Still, this opinion is scientifically improbable. To those inquirers who are particularly interested in the question of evolution, the instructor may devote a special session or two or recommend such works as Windle's "The Church and Science" and Archbishop Sheehan's "Apologetics and Christian Doctrine."

CHAPTER XV.

ORIGINAL SIN

A SIMPLE ILLUSTRATION

In order to explain to you, my dear friend, the Catholic doctrine of original sin (a doctrine taught also by many Protestant denominations, at least in the earlier stage of their existence), I am going to give you a simple example or illustration. Many object that this doctrine is against God's justice. How can God, they ask, justly punish us for a sin that Adam committed thousands and thousands of years ago? (By the way, we don't know how long ago our first parents were created. The Bible gives us no definite data, and the Church has made no pronouncement on this matter. The human race may be six, eight, ten, twelve thousand years old—its age does not effect Catholic doctrine.)

Here is an easy example to illustrate original sin. A certain splendid concert was arranged. Star singers of international fame were to take part; the best actors in the world were going to perform; the finest pianists and violinists known were to play. The program was magnificent, and the tickets of admission were very costly—front seats, twenty dollars, back seats, ten dollars.

In the city where the great concert was to be held a certain man, James Stanwell, was working for a wealthy man named William Astor. Stanwell was receiving $100 a week, was paying $20 a week rent, and had a wife and seven children to support. A short time before the concert Astor invited Stanwell into his office and thus addressed him: "I know, James, that yourself and your wife and children would be delighted to attend the forthcoming concert, and so I have bought nine front seat tickets for you. They are a gift from me to you and your family. The only condition I lay down for you before you receive them is that for the next few days you take the place of Dickens in driving one of our trucks. This work will be no heavier than your present duties, but since you are a good driver, I am asking you to relieve Dickens, who is ill. Dickens is receiving the same salary as yourself."

After a day or two Stanwell got tired of his new job and objected to continue driving the truck. He walked into Astor's office and said truculently: "Look here; I've had enough of this truck-driving. I refuse to do any more of it. Get someone else."

"Very well, James," replied Mr. Astor, "since you refuse to do this particular work which I gave you and laid down as a condition for your receiving the nine tickets to the concert, I now withdraw your gift. Neither yourself nor your family will receive a ticket. However, I'll not be too hard on you; you may go back to your former work and I shall continue to give you the usual $100 a week."

No one could reasonably accuse William Astor of acting unjustly towards James Stanwell. Nor could Astor be reasonably accused of acting unjustly towards Stanwell's wife and children, from whom he withdrew or withheld the tickets for the grand concert, for those tickets were a free gift on his part, and consequently he was perfectly free to lay down the condition he did.

APPLICATION OF THIS EXAMPLE

In this parable William Astor represents God, James Stanwell represents Adam, and Stanwell's family represents ourselves—Adam's descendants. The nine tickets represent the supernatural gifts—gifts of grace—which God bestowed on Adam and intended to pass on to Adam's descendants. The weekly salary of $100 a week represents the gifts or faculties of Nature —what are called natural gifts or endowments.

God laid down one special condition for Adam if he was to keep the supernatural life for himself and transmit it to his descendants, viz., that he should not eat the fruit of one particular tree in the Garden of Eden. But Adam wilfully disobeyed God and thus forfeited for himself and for us, his descendants, the gift of the supernatural life, which consists especially in what is called **sanctifying grace,** and of which I spoke in our last chat.

Adam committed a **personal sin** by his deliberate disobedience, but we, his children, did not do so, for we were not yet born. Yet Adam, as the head of the whole human race, represented us or stood for us and acted in our name, so that, in a sense, we all sinned in Adam. According to God's wish, we should all have come into this world with our souls adorned with sanctifying grace; we should all have been born in a state of grace, which we would have had from the moment of conception. Of course, any individual might have later sinned and lost grace for himself and his own descendants. But, had Adam remained faithful, the human race as such would have remained on that high plane of the supernatural life.

The absence of grace from our soul, which grace should be there and would be there but for Adam's disobedience, is like a blot or stain on our soul, and is known as **original sin.**

91

TEMPTATION OF ADAM

The Bible tells us that Adam and Eve were tempted before they fell. Yes, the devil, an evil spirit, a fallen angel, tempted them. He appeared to Eve as a shining serpent and talked her into disobeying God, and she in turn talked Adam into committing sin.

Before creating man, God had created countless pure spirits—spirits who were not united to bodies. They are called **Angels**. They, too, were put to the test by God. The majority obeyed and were at once rewarded by the everlasting vision and love and enjoyment of God; that is, they were at once admitted to **heaven**. But a large number disobeyed through pride and were cast away into everlasting punishment, which we call **hell**.

If we commit a serious sin—a mortal sin—and die in that state, we also shall be condemned to hell. Had Adam and Eve died without repentance, they would also have been condemned to hell, which consists essentially in the eternal loss of God, the eternal separation from God. There are other pains of hell—secondary pains—of which you will be told in due time.

TRINITY, INCARNATION, REDEMPTION

God has revealed to us that in Him there are three Persons, really distinct and yet equal in all the perfections of the Godhead: the Father, the Son, and the Holy Ghost. This truth, which we firmly believe because God has taught it, is known as the mystery of the Blessed **Trinity**.

A **person** is a complete, individual, intellectual nature that possesses or governs itself. A stone or tree or dog is not a person because it is not intellectual or rational. A human body or a human soul alone is not a person, because each is an incomplete nature, and even the two united in a complete human nature do not constitute a person unless that complete nature possesses itself and is master of its actions. Thus the human nature of Christ, although complete and perfect, is not a human person, for, as we shall see, it is possessed or governed by a Divine Person. A person is said to be the "center of attribution," which simply means that all the actions and sufferings of a nature are ascribed or attributed to the person that possesses it. As regards free acts, the person governing the nature from which those acts proceed is **responsible** for them. Two other terms, which express in reality the same thing as nature, are **essence** and **substance**.

Now, in God there is only one essence or substance, but that one Divine Nature is possessed by three distinct Persons; each of which can say I; each of which is the centre of attribution to which all the operations of the Divine Nature are ascribed.

God the Son, while remaining God, took unto Himself a human nature, which He possessed and governed as His very own from the first instant of its existence. That is the meaning of the **Incarnation.** He thus became our great High Priest and Victim in order to offer to God the Father a sacrifice of infinite atonement and infinite value for the redemption of mankind.

To **redeem** means to **buy** back. By His sacrifice offered on the Cross, Jesus rescued us from the slavery of the devil and reinstated us in the friendship of God; on Calvary He offered Himself as a victim of atonement and ransom for the entire human race. Calvary is the Sacrifice of Redemption. You will be told more about sacrifice when we come to the doctrine of the Mass.

A Divine Person offering a sacrifice of infinite

value in His human nature, and thus making more
than abundant satisfaction for the sin of Adam and
the sins of mankind, and paying more than an abundant price to buy back for us the priceless gifts of
grace—of sanctifying grace, faith, hope, and charity
with their accompanying treasures, and actual grace,
and eternal glory, which consists in the beatific vision or the face to face vision of God for eternity!
That is what is meant by Redemption.

But what are called the **preternatural** gifts of
our first parents—freedom from death, suffering, ignorance, and the lust of the flesh—were not restored
to mankind by the Sacrifice of Redemption. But
these gifts are almost as nothing in comparison with
the unspeakable gift of the **supernatural** life merited
for us by Christ, to procure which ineffable treasure
we adults must freely, by divine grace, surrender
ourselves to God's sweet claims.

CHAPTER XVI.

GRACE AND THE SACRAMENTS

IN our previous chats, my dear convert, I have more than once mentioned **grace** and have briefly explained it. Before proceeding further, I shall enlarge that explanation.

All grace is a supernatural gift. I have told you that **supernatural** means above or beyond the powers or claims of nature. Grace is a wondrous gift bestowed on us quite freely by God in order to make us holy or Godlike. I have already mentioned **sanctifying grace.** This is a marvellous quality which God puts in our soul, making us His own adopted children and giving us a passport or ticket, as it were, to the eternal vision and love and enjoyment of Himself. Sanctifying grace mirrors God in the human soul and makes it a sharer, in some mysterious manner, of God's own nature. A person who has this gift is said to be in the **state of grace.** Once we receive this supernal gift, we retain it unless we commit a mortal sin—a serious or grievous offence against God. And, as soon as we get God's forgiveness (about which I shall speak later), sanctifying grace returns to the soul—the return of this gift and God's forgiveness are simultaneous; that is, they occur together, for they are inseparable.

There is another gift called **actual grace.** This is a passing gift, given to our soul in order to help us to overcome temptation, to practice virtue, etc. It is given to our mind or will or heart, or it may consist in God's lifting or removing us, as it were, from dangerous circumstances and placing us in circumstances where we easily please Him. It is a flash of heavenly light shining on our mind; an impulse given to our will; a quelling of our passions or the arousing of holy emotions. We need this grace to keep from sin and to practice virtue. "Without me," said Christ to His Apostles, "you can do nothing." Above all, we need actual grace in order to perform supernatural acts—acts that will merit for us an increase of sanctifying grace and thus augment our glory in heaven.

This short account of sanctifying and actual grace will suffice for you for the present. I am now going to tell you about one of the great means of getting God's grace. There are two effective means—**Prayer and the Sacraments.** Prayer is easy to understand; even a pagan grasps the meaning of it. You may simply read through the chapter in the Catechism on Prayer or read some little Catholic book on the subject. I am now giving you a **Catechism,** which I want you to read carefully. It is an excellent summary of Catholic doctrine, and it will recall to your mind many of the truths we have chatted over and impress them more deeply in your mind.

But the Sacraments are more difficult to understand than Prayer; at least, they require more explanation, and to an inquirer or catechumen, who is already familiar with prayer, the Sacraments appear often to be something new. So I shall explain them in this chat.

MEANING OF A SACRAMENT

A sacrament is a visible sign instituted by Christ to give grace. You know well, of course, what is meant by a sign. Of its nature a sign is something visible;

hence this adjective is given in the definition just to explain what is already contained in the idea of a sign. We use many signs in our everyday life. A handshake is a sign of friendship; laughter is a sign of amusement; the flag is a sign of patriotism; the lily is a sign (or symbol) of purity; the heart is a sign (or symbol) of love. A sign or symbol is essentially something visible, and it generally stands for or signifies something that is invisible. Every word we utter is really a sign of an idea, which is something invisible in our mind.

SIGNS CHOSEN BY OUR LORD

Grace is an invisible gift of God—something supernatural which directly affects the soul. Now, Christ willed to give us certain signs or symbols to show that grace was being poured into our soul; signs, in fact, which, according to His institution, actually produce grace in the soul.

Suppose you wished to choose a sign of purification or cleansing, what would you naturally select? I think you would choose water and the action of washing. Well, Christ wished to show that our soul was being cleansed from the stain of original sin, and He chose water and the action of washing.

To Nicodemus Our Lord declared: "Unless a man be born again of water and the Holy Ghost, he cannot enter the kingdom of God" (John iii., 5). And in His last address or final commission to the Apostles He said: "Go, teach all nations . . . baptizing them in the name of the Father and of the Son and of the Holy Ghost" (Matt. xxviii., 19). The word **baptize** means **wash.** Thus **Baptism** is a spiritual or supernatural washing—a cleansing of the soul from the stain of original sin. And, since sanctifying grace makes us adopted children of God, we are said to be born again or regenerated by Baptism. That is why it is sometimes called the Sacrament of Regeneration.

In eastern countries it was customary for sportsmen—wrestlers, boxers, boatmen, etc.—to rub their muscles with oil in order to strengthen them before entering a contest. Thus oil or anointing was a sign or symbol of imparting strength, and therefore that sign has been chosen for the sacrament which imparts supernatural strength or courage to a regenerated soul. The sacrament of strength is known as **Confirmation,** and it is given by a bishop, who lays his hand on the head of the person to be confirmed and marks that person's forehead with chrism (a mixture of olive oil and balsam), while he utters certain words expressing the grace and effect of the sacrament.

Oil was used in the east also for healing wounds, and Christ chose it as the sign of healing the soul. There is a sacrament for persons in danger of death from sickness, and that sacrament is called **Extreme Unction, which means the Last Anointing.** It is given by anointing the senses with olive oil while suitable words or prayers are said to express the grace of the sacrament. You will find this sacrament explicitly mentioned in the Epistle of St. James (v. 14 and 15).

The laying on of hands (imposition of hands) was chosen especially as the sign or symbol for conferring the power of the priesthood. A suitable prayer accompanies this ceremony. The sacrament which gives sacred ministers (deacons), priests, and bishops to the Church is called **Holy Orders.**

Marriage is a solemn, natural contract known even to pagans. Our Lord simply raised this contract to the level of a sacrament, so that, if two baptized persons enter this contract, they necessarily receive the sacrament of **Matrimony**, which, like every sacrament, gives special grace.

TWO SACRAMENTS TO BE EXPLAINED IN DETAIL

What I have said is a simple summary of the Church's teaching about sacraments. You can read more about each sacrament in the Catechism which I have just now given you. But I am going to chat with you at great length about two sacraments in particular—**Penance** and the **Eucharist**. Penance is the Sacrament of Forgiveness; the Holy Eucharist is the Sacrament of Love. The Sacrament of Forgiveness or Mercy is administered in the form of a judgment. The priest is the divinely appointed judge and the sinner is both the accused and the accuser. The Sacrament of Love is the Sacrament of the Body and Blood of Christ, which our Savior, in His boundless love, gave us as the very nourishment of our soul. And, because this Sacrament is spiritual nourishment, Christ chose to give it to us under the outward forms of bread and wine. But I shall not deal with these two sacraments just now, for I am going to give you a number of talks about them. In our next chat I shall commence to tell you about the Blessed Eucharist, the Sacrament of the Body and Blood of Christ.

CHANNELS OF GRACE

In the present chat, my dear catechumen, you have learned what a sacrament is and also that there are seven sacraments: Baptism, Confirmation, Eucharist, Penance, Holy Orders, Matrimony, and Extreme Unction.

In our chat on Redemption I told you that God the Son, who became man for love of us, redeemed us by His passion and death—by offering Himself as a Victim on Calvary, by which offering or sacrifice He made infinite satisfaction for all our sins and merited for us more than abundant grace. He stored up for us infinite treasures of grace by His supreme sacrifice of love. It is as if He excavated an immense, a measureless reservoir or lake, filled with inexhaustible heavenly waters. In order to convey those living waters of grace to our parched, thirsting, sin-stained souls, He invented or devised seven celestial channels or pipes through which purifying, refreshing, invigorating streams might flow from that supernal lake. Those seven divine channels are the sacraments. Thus you see, my dear friend, how precious a gift to our fallen race is the sacramental system devised by a merciful, loving Savior.

CHAPTER XVII.

THE REAL PRESENCE TAUGHT IN SCRIPTURE

THE Catholic Church teaches that in the Blessed Sacrament—the Sacrament of the Eucharist—the body and blood of Jesus Christ are truly, really, and substantially present under the appearances or form or accidents of bread and wine. Let us go to the Gospel and see what Christ Himself has explicitly told us of this mystery; I mean what has been written down of His teaching concerning this truth, for, as I have already told you, my dear friend, and proved, all that Christ said is not recorded in the New Testament.

We read that Our Lord first promised most clearly that He would give us His real flesh to eat and His real blood to drink, and that later, on the night before He was crucified, He changed bread and wine into His own body and blood, and gave His priests power to do so.

LITERAL AND FIGURATIVE

This wonderful promise is recorded in the sixth chapter of St. John. I shall read it to you; it is expressed in the passages from verse 48 to verse 70.

Now, before proceeding further, let me speak of two ways in which words may be used, or of two different senses or meanings in which we may use words or expressions. These two senses are called **literal** and **figurative.** If, for instance, I tell you that, when out hunting, I shot a fox, you know that I mean a real fox, that I am using this word in its natural or literal meaning. But, if I advise you to be careful in your dealings with Tim Tongiorgi, adding that he is a fox, you will understand that I am not using this word in its literal meaning; but in a transferred or **figurative** meaning; that I am only comparing Tim to a fox because he is sly and cunning, like that animal.

There are several figures of speech; two well-known figures are called **similes** and **metaphors.** When we say Will Calvin is **like** a bear, we are using a simile; when we say he **is** a bear, we are employing a metaphor. To speak in similes or metaphors is to speak **figuratively;** when a person has used metaphors alone, we say he has spoken **metaphorically,** although we might say even then that he spoke figuratively, for every metaphor is a figure of speech.

Sometimes Christ spoke metaphorically, e.g., when He called Herod a fox, when He called Himself the vine and the Apostles the branches, when He referred to Himself as the door. Generally, however, He spoke literally. I shall give you two simple rules—though they are not the only ones—to help you in determining whether Christ spoke literally or metaphorically. These two rules refer to circumstances in which a doubt or dispute arose about His statement.

(1) When Jesus spoke figuratively, and His hearers understood Him literally because they were either simple-minded or ignorant, His custom was to explain His true meaning. And even when there is no record of Christ having done this, St. John is noted for doing so.

(2) When Christ spoke literally and His hearers showed displeasure and objected, He was accustomed to insist more strongly or emphatically on His literal meaning.

Let me illustrate these rules. As for the first, the example of Nicodemus is a striking case. Our Lord had declared that a man must be **born again**. Nicodemus wondered at this and asked **how** could a man be born again when he was already old. At once Christ explained that He did not mean physical rebirth, but spiritual regeneration. "Unless a man be born again of water and the Holy Ghost," etc. (John iii. 5). ، Another illustration is the example given in the sixteenth chapter of St. Matthew. Our Lord said to the Apostles: "Beware of the **leaven** of the pharisees and sadducees." The Apostles understood Him literally and began to discuss this warning. But Christ at once explained His meaning: "Why do you not understand that it was not concerning **bread** that I spoke to you?" (vv. 5-12). A third example I take from the eighth chapter of St. John. When Jesus told His Apostles that Lazarus was **asleep** and they understood Him literally, He at once explained His metaphor by stating simply: "Lazarus is **dead**" (vv. 11-14).

As regard the second rule I have mentioned, we see it exemplified in various cases. Take, for example, the incident narrated in the ninth chapter of St. Matthew. When Christ told the man sick of the palsy that his sins were forgiven, he spoke literally and the scribes understood Him literally. They accused Him of blasphemy. Then Christ repeated more forcibly His claim of power to forgive sins and worked a miracle to prove it. Another instance of the rule is found in the eighth chapter of St. John Our Lord stated that Abraham rejoiced to see His day. The Jews objected: "Thou are not yet fifty years of age, and hast Thou seen Abraham?" Whereupon Christ repeated more emphatically His literal meaning: "Amen, amen, I say to you: Before Abraham was made, I am" (vv. 56-58).

THE GREAT PROMISE—LITERAL MEANING CLEAR

Let us now consider Christ's promise to give us His flesh and blood and apply to them the two rules we have considered. Here are Christ's own words:

"I am the bread of life. Your fathers ate manna in the desert, and they are dead. This is the bread that cometh down from heaven; that if anyone eat of it he may not die. I am the living bread that came down from heaven. If anyone eat of this bread, he shall live for ever; and the bread that I will give is my flesh for the life of the world" (John vi., 48-52).

Mark especially the words: **The bread that I will give is my flesh.** Did Christ utter these words in a literal or a figurative sense? Here we have a splendid chance to apply the two rules I have elaborated.

The Jews certainly understood Christ's words literally; they understood Him to mean His **real flesh.** They even began at once to argue as to how Christ could give His true flesh to eat. "The Jews therefore strove among themselves, saying: How can this man give us His flesh to eat?" (v. 53).

Their question began with the same word as that of Nicodemus—**How?** Will Our Lord now explain, as He did to Nicodemus, that He is speaking metaphorically? Will He declare that He does not intend to give His real flesh, but only a sign or representation of it? Yes, according to His custom, if He is not speaking literally. But, if He is speaking literally, He will, according to His custom, repeat His literal meaning still more forcibly. And this is exactly what Christ did:

"Then Jesus said to them: Amen, amen, I say to you; unless you eat the flesh of the Son of Man and drink His blood, you shall not have life in you. He that eateth my flesh and drinketh my blood hath everlasting life, and I will raise him up on the last day.

For my flesh is meat indeed, and my blood is drink indeed. He that eateth my flesh and drinketh my blood abideth in me as I in him" (vv. 54-56).

Jesus continued a little longer, but the crowd refused to believe him. He had made it quite clear that He intended to give His real flesh and His real blood, but they would not believe **because they could not understand.** They refused to make an **act of faith.**

"After this many of His disciples went back, and they walked no more with Him" (v. 67).

Christ saw them going; He allowed them to depart; they had rightly understood Him, and so He refused to give them any further explanation. If he had been speaking figuratively of His body and blood, He would have called those people back and explained. We should notice, too, that Our Lord here enacted a very serious law; His grave words show that. Now, in making important laws, legislators do not employ metaphors—they express the law in clear, literal terms. And that is precisely what Christ did on this solemn occasion.

Then Jesus turned to the twelve Apostles and asked: "Will you also go away?" The Apostles did not understand any better than those who had departed how their Divine Master was going to give His flesh and blood as food and drink. **But they believed it because Jesus had said it. They had faith.** So at once Peter answered in the name of all the Apostles:

"Lord, to whom shall we go? Thou hast the words of eternal life. And we have believed and have known that Thou art Christ, the Son of God" (vv. 69 and 70).

PROMISE FULFILLED AT THE LAST SUPPER

Twelve months had elapsed since Jesus had spoken those wonderful words at Capharnaum (Capernaum), and He was now seated with His loved Apostles at supper for the last time in His mortal life. He was about to die on the morrow for love of us; but He would first fulfil the marvellous promise He had made. Let us listen to St. Matthew as he narrates for us in his simple, beautiful style the institution of the Holy Eucharist:

"Whilst they were at supper, Jesus took bread and blessed it and broke it and gave it to His disciples and said: Take ye and eat. This is my body.

And taking the chalice, He gave thanks and gave to them, saying: "Drink ye all of this. For this is My blood of the New Testament, which shall be shed for many unto the remission of sins" (XXVI., 26-28).

Christ's words could not be clearer. He did not say: Here is my Body; or: With this is My Body; or: This is a sign or a figure of a representation of My Body; or: This represents My Body. No, He declared simply and clearly: **This is My Body.** And we Catholics say, with a firm faith, as Peter did at Capernaum: "Lord, to whom shall we go? Thou hast the words of eternal life. And we have believed and have known that Thou art Christ, the Son of God. We firmly believe that Thou givest us Thy real Body and Thy real Blood, because Thou hast said: This is my body; this is my blood."

Note, too, that at the last Supper Christ made His last will and testament. When a dying person makes his will, he uses no vague or poetical or figurative language; no, he expresses himself clearly and unmistakably in literal terms. And this is just what Christ did when He made His last will and testament: "This is My Body. This is My Blood of the New Testament."

TEACHING OF ST. PAUL

In his first Epistle to the Corinthians, St. Paul clearly teaches the doctrine of Christ's real presence in the Eucharist. After narrating the words of institution, the Apostle continues: "Therefore whosoever shall eat this bread or drink the chalice of the Lord unworthily shall be guilty of the Body and Blood of the Lord" (XI., 27). But how could one be guilty of the very Body and Blood of Christ if he partook merely of a piece of bread or a sup of wine? It is certain, then, that St. Paul taught that we receive in Holy Communion the real body and the real blood of Christ.

In the same Epistle St. Paul asks: "The chalice of benediction which we bless, is it not the Communion of the Blood of Christ? And the bread which we break, is it not the partaking of the Body of the Lord?" (X., 16).

ST. PAUL'S TEXT CORRUPTED

In the Authorized Version (Protestant English version of James I.), the first passage I have quoted from St. Paul was deliberately corrupted by the translators, for they saw that St. Paul allowed Communion under either kind—under the form of bread or under the form of wine—and that the Apostle taught that, under either kind, we receive both the Body and Blood of Christ. The so-called Reformers objected to this Catholic doctrine, and so they changed the word **or into and,** or rather, they gave a wrong translation of the Greek conjunction. (This Epistle was written in Greek.) But they were only fifteen centuries too late! The Bible had been faithfully copied all that time and faithfully translated into many languages. So glaring was the corruption inserted in the Authorized Version (of King James), that the Revised Version (of Queen Victoria) has corrected it and inserted the word **or.**

Now, my dear friend, I have given you a full instruction—a fairly long chat—on the Real Presence, which I have clearly proved from the Sacred Scriptures.

CHAPTER XVIII.

THE REAL PRESENCE TAUGHT BY THE FATHERS

IN our last chat, my dear friend, I proved to you from the Scriptures that Christ's body and blood are truly, really, and substantially present in the Blessed Sacrament under the appearances or form of bread and wine. To-day I am going to prove this doctrine from Tradition. I have already explained to you that there are two pure, absolutely unadulterated sources or founts of God's revealed truth, viz., Sacred Scripture and Divine Tradition. One clear indication of revealed truths contained in Tradition, though not expressly recorded in Scripture, is the **testimony of the Fathers.**

From the death of the Apostles to the present time there have been numberless scholars who have written books of defence and explanation of the Catholic Faith. Those great writers, many of whom were saints, who lived during the early ages of Christianity, are called the **Fathers of the Church.** They had at their disposal or in their hands, besides the Sacred Scriptures, with which they were most conversant, the full Tradition, the rich legacy, of doctrine freshly received from the Apostles themselves, or from those who closely followed the Apostles.

The writings of the early Fathers are very important, for they clearly testify to the doctrines believed by the Universal Church from the earliest times.

Still, we cannot reasonably ask our converts to make anything like an exhaustive study of the writings of the Fathers. Indeed, the average Catholic has only an elementary knowledge of them, and, in fact, of only a few of them. But I have met not a few inquirers and converts who showed great interest in this early testimony to our faith. One of these converts was a young Scotsman, the son of a Presbyterian minister of Glasgow. This young man followed, at his own wish, a long course of instruction before I received him into the Church. Then his own Presbyterian family disowned him and soon the Catholic young lady to whom he was engaged gave him up because he could not get a suitable position at the time. But the young Scots convert never wavered in the Catholic faith or in the faithful practice of it, for he had a thorough, intelligent grasp of our holy religion. He drank in every chat; he read the books I lent him, especially "The Sincere Christian" by Dr. Hay (one of the best books I have ever seen on Catholic doctrine proved from Scripture); and he took a keen interest in the writings of the early Fathers which I brought under his notice. He was an ordinary working man, and I feel that many a prospective convert could follow an equally thorough course extending over a period of six months.

Well, my dear friend, in the course of our chats I shall give you at least some quotations of early Fathers to support certain doctrines which non-Catholics repudiate. Clear texts of Scripture, reinforced by striking statements of early Fathers, should appeal to every unbiased mind and convince it. I could give you also the particular authentic sources from which I take the various extracts of the early Fathers; but this would be burdening you unnecessarily, for I could not reasonably ask you to study the works referred to.

If you do wish at any time particularly to verify some striking quotation from some Father, I shall gladly oblige you.

THE EARLY FATHERS AND THE REAL PRESENCE

To the average convert I am generally content to give the testimonies of six of the early Fathers regarding the Real Presence of Christ in the Holy Eucharist. These six Fathers were Bishops of important Sees in the early ages of Christianity; three of them lived in the east, three in the west. Their writings, then, testify to the universal faith of the early Christians.

The six scholars and bishops to whom I refer are: (1) St. Cyril of Jerusalem (born in the year 315, died in 386); (2) St. John Chrysostom, of Constantinople, the Christian Demosthenes (347-407); (3) St. Cyril of Alexandria (died 444); (4) St. Cyprian, of Carthage (died 258); (5) St. Augustine of Hippo (354-430); (6) St. Ambrose, of Milan (340-397).

I shall now quote a passage or two from the writings of each of these Fathers. The words I give are, of course, but a translation (though a correct one) of the original statements.

ST. CYRIL OF JERUSALEM

"Since He declared and said of the bread, 'This is My body', who will dare henceforth to doubt? And since He also so emphatically said, 'This is my blood', who will ever doubt, so as to say that it is not His blood?

"Formerly He changed water into wine at Cana of Galilee . . . and shall we consider it unworthy to believe of Him that He changed wine into His blood?

". . . For under the appearance of bread He gives

us His body, and under the appearance of wine He gives us His Blood; so that, when you receive, you relish the body and blood of Christ, being made partaker of that same body and blood. For thus we become **Christ-bearers** (carriers of Christ), that is, **bearing Christ in our bodies. . . .**

"Do not regard these things as mere bread and mere wine; for they are the body and blood of Christ. For, although your sense tell you this, let your faith strengthen you. Do not judge this by your taste; but let your faith make you **certain beyond all doubt** that you become worthy to be made **partakers of the body and blood of Christ."**

ST. JOHN CHRYSOSTOM

"What is in the chalice is that very thing which flowed from His side, and we are made partakers of it. . . . This is that body which was covered with blood, and pierced with a spear, which poured forth saving streams of blood and water. . . . **He gave us this body to hold and to eat, and this is a proof of intense love. . . .**

"How many people now say: 'I wish I could see His form, His figure, His clothes, His shoes'! Behold, you do see Him, you touch Him, you eat Him. And you, indeed, wish to see His clothes; but **He allows you not only to see, but also to eat, and to touch, and to receive Him within you."**

ST. CYRIL OF ALEXANDRIA

"He said in a demonstrative way, 'This is my body', and 'This is my blood', in order that you may not think that those things which are seen are a figure (or type), but that, in some mysterious manner, **they are changed by Almighty God into the body and blood of Christ in truth. . . .**

"For just as, if anyone puts more wax into melted wax, one wax becomes mixed with the other, so a person who receives the flesh and blood of the Lord is so joined with Him that Christ is found in this person, and this person is Christ."

ST. CYPRIAN

"We must give Communion so that those whom we stir up and exhort to battle we may not leave unarmed and naked, but may fortify them with the protection of the blood and body of Christ. . . . For how can we teach them to **shed their own blood** in the confession of His name if we refuse them, when about to fight, **the blood of Christ?**"

ST. AUGUSTINE OF HIPPO

"Christ was carried in His own hands when, committing His own body, He said, 'This is my body'. For **He carried that body in His own hands.**"

ST. AMBROSE

"Perhaps you may say: 'I see something different; how can you tell me that I receive the body of Christ?' . . . Let us prove that this is not what nature formed, but what the blessing has consecrated; and that the force of the blessing is greater than that of nature. . . . If the word of Elias was so powerful as to bring forth fire from heaven, shall not the word of Christ be able to **change** the species of the elements?"

A disciple of St. Ambrose wrote a book on the Sacraments. From this treatise I take but one short passage: "This bread is bread before the words of the Sacrament; **when the consecration is added, from bread it is made the flesh of Christ.**"

Thus you see, my dear convert, how clearly the early Fathers, who had received their doctrine fresh and pure from the Apostles, taught the very same doctrine as the Catholic Church does to-day about the real presence of Christ in the Holy Eucharist—that the bread and wine are truly changed by the words of consecration (the words of Christ) into the very body and blood of Jesus Christ.

THE "APPEARANCES" OF BREAD AND WINE

Notice, my dear friend, that the Fathers stress the fact that the **appearances** of bread and wine remain after the bread and wine have been changed into the body and blood of Christ. By the appearances, which are also called **accidents,** we mean the color, shape, flavor, weight, hardness or softness, etc. In every creature we distinguish between **substance** and **accidents.** Since we are concerned here with visible things, I shall give a few examples taken from material things around us.

Ice-cream may have the flavor of vanilla or chocolate. The flavor is a mere accident. Ice-cream may have different colors . The color, too, is an accident. What remains the same under these outward appearances—of flavor and color—is called the substance. The substance of a thing is the substratum of that thing—what remains permanent or underlying or unchanged under the external modifications or accidents. A piece of wax may be shaped as a cube or a sphere or a cylinder; its shape is a mere accident. It may be solid or liquid (when melted). Its hardness or softness is an accident. What remains permanent under those successive changes is the substance of the wax. John Lindsay was once a small boy with rosy cheeks and black hair. Now he is an old man with a wrinkled face and grey hair or no hair. His size, color or complexion, kind of hair, weight, etc., are but accidents; the substance of John Lindsay remains the same.

Now when bread and wine are changed by God's omnipotence into the body and blood of Christ the substance of the bread and wine completely vanishes in order to make way for the substance of the body and blood of Christ which instantly succeeds it—or, rather, the two acts or effects are simultaneous. But, although the body and blood of Christ are now truly, really, and substantially present, the accidents of bread and wine—the size, weight, color, flavor, solid or liquid condition—remain. These accidents or appearances are kept in existence solely by God's almighty power—they should have completely disappeared with the substances which supported them. It is only by a miracle that they continue.

The change of bread and wine into the body and blood of Christ is called **transubstantiation.** It is a miracle and a mystery, but we firmly believe this truth because Christ Himself has said: "This is My body. This is My blood." Such was the faith of the Apostles; such was the faith of the early Fathers and the entire Church of the early centuries; such has ever been the faith of Christ's Church down to the present year; such will ever be the faith of the Church till the end of the world. A great Anglican convert, Frederick William Faber, has beautifully written:

"Jesus, my Lord, my God, my all!
  How can I love Thee as I ought?
And how revere this wondrous gift,
  So far surpassing hope or thought?
Sweet Sacrament, we Thee adore,
Oh, make us love Thee more and more."

CHAPTER XIX.

SACRIFICE

CHRIST gave us the great gift of His body and blood not only as the food of our souls (which we receive in Holy Communion, about which I shall tell you in due time), but also as our daily sacrifice. This Holy Sacrifice is called the Mass, the Eucharistic Sacrifice, the Clean Oblation, the Unbloody Sacrifice, the Adorable Sacrifice. Since the central act of our worship of God, the very heart of our religion, is the Eucharistic Sacrifice, and you will, after you become a Catholic, assist frequently, at least every Sunday, at this tremendous Sacrifice, I intend to give you several instructions, my dear friend, on the Mass, for the better you grasp this sublime oblation, the more will you appreciate it, and the oftener will you assist at it or take part with the priest in offering it. Let me begin by explaining to you the idea of sacrifice, which is found even in pagan religions and was positively prescribed by God to His chosen people in the Old Testament.

MEANING OF SACRIFICE

The idea of a **gift** underlies sacrifice, or is bound up with it. Everyone, even a child, knows what a gift is. The greatest savages easily perceive the meaning of gifts and bestow them accordingly. Now, a gift may be offered or given for various reasons. We might offer a gift to some high dignitary in order to honor him

—to express our appreciation of his dignity and to show that we duly respect and revere him. Or we might send a gift to someone in order to show our gratitude for some favor or favors received. We might give a present or gift also to placate or appease one whom we have insulted or offended—to express thereby our sincere apology and ask pardon for the grief we caused. Again, we might offer a gift to someone with influence in order to procure a favor we desired. These are simple examples which anyone at all can understand.

Thus a gift may be given (1) to honor a person in high office, (2) to show our thankfulness to a benefactor, (3) to express apology or sorrow for an offence and seek reconciliation, (4) to procure favors we desire.

Well, my dear friend, there you have the idea of **sacrifice** put in a simple, elementary way, although that idea needs to be expanded or explained more fully. Before doing so, however, I may say that the matter might be summarized by stating that we generally understand a gift as **an expression of love.** And, in regard to God, to whom adoration, thanksgiving, atonement or satisfaction, and petition are due (the very four acts I have already illustrated), love includes these four acts. God is infinite Goodness, and so He is worthy of our supreme or highest love. And love of God certainly of itself prompts us to give Him those four acts of worship which ordinary right reason prescribes. It is easier to explain sacrifice by considering God's goodness as the object of our love.

Sacrifice might be described as the public worship of God expressed in sign or symbol. Ordinarily we pray to God by word or even thought. But we may pray to Him also by sign. Thus merely to kneel in spirit in His presence is equivalent to saying: "My

Creator and my God, I adore Thee." Our public prayers—I mean those said in the name of the community (what may be termed social prayers)—are expressed in certain words which are said aloud by a group of persons or by one person praying in their name. But sacrifice is more than such public or social prayer. It is a public **action** whereby a **gift** is officially, or in the name of the community or society, offered to God to express the worship of the entire community. Sacrifice might also be described as the public offering of a gift of love to the Deity. But I must explain these things in detail.

THREE THINGS REQUIRED IN SACRIFICE

Since sacrifice is an act of public worship—the greatest expression, in fact, of public worship—there must be someone elected or appointed or designated to act in this matter in the name of the people. This person is called a **priest.** Besides, there must be a **gift**—something precious or a sign of something precious—to be offered to God. The most precious thing we possess is our own life, and so some object that represents in some way human life, or is closely associated with it, has always been chosen by various races—God's chosen people (who were directed by God Himself) and different pagan peoples—to be offered to God in sacrifice. Besides the priest and the gift, there must be an **altar.** By this we generally understand something constructed (and as a rule neatly or nicely or exquisitely constructed) on which the gift is publicly laid by the priest, in the name of the people. The altar is considered to represent or symbolize the Deity, who receives the gift.

When the priest who acts in the name of the people puts the gift on the altar with a certain ceremony or holy action, the object offered passes at once from the possession of the people into the hands of God and thereby becomes holy or sacred or consecrated. In fact, the verb **sacrifice** literally means **make sacred,** and the noun means the action whereby a thing is rendered sacred, or the thing itself that is made sacred by such action.

The history of sacrifice—whether amongst the Jewish people or amongst pagans—tells us that mankind has been accustomed to offer the Deity two kinds of gifts—always, however, connected in some way with human life. The inanimate gifts offered were corn, oil, flour, bread, wine, first fruits of the harvest, etc. The animate (or living) gifts were sheep, lambs, calves, heifers, etc. The gift offered symbolized human life, and by publicly and officially offering such gifts the people wished to express in the language of sign or symbol that they thereby dedicated, or rather consecrated, or gave back to God their own life, which they had received from Him. This thought could be beautifully developed, but I must confine myself to a simple chat and not launch into a long disquisition.

When a living gift was offered, the animal, called a **victim,** was generally slain. Then its blood (which especially or particularly represented the life of the animal) was poured out on the altar, or at the foot of the altar, by the priest, and the body of the animal was roasted or even burnt in order to express, as it were, that the people were offering God a repast. Often, having made the offering of the blood and the roasted animal, the priest and the people partook of the meat as if at a heavenly festival to which God had invited them. We might term this ceremony **Communion with God.**

Another reason why animals were slain was that the people, recognizing themselves as sinners, wished to show that they merited death—and were willing to undergo death—for their sins. Since they could not lawfully put themselves to death, they killed an animal in their stead as an expression of their sorrow for sin and their desire to expiate their offences They transferred, as it were, their own sins to the animal, or rather the punishment deserved by their own transgressions. The slaying of the victim and the offering of its blood to God in atonement was an emphatic manner of expressing their sincere repentance and their desire to be reconciled with their Creator and expiate or satisfy for their sins as far as possible.

Thus, considering their sins, they offered God a **blood-stained gift,** as a repentant child might offer **his** offended father a **tear-stained** gift.

SUMMARY OF THE NOTION OF SACRIFICE

Before I come to the great Sacrifice of the New Testament (the Sacrifice of the New Law or the Christian Dispensation), I shall give you, my dear friend, a summary of what I have said about sacrifice:

1. We may pray not only by words, but also by signs, just as we may express our thoughts and feelings by signs as well as by words

2. A **gift** is a sign or token of love, and so we may express our love for God by offering Him a gift.

3. Worship of God comprises four acts: **Adoration, thanksgiving, satisfaction** (or atonement), and **petition.**

4. The highest act of public worship is **sacrifice.**

5. Sacrifice is the offering made to God by a priest, in the name of the people, of a gift which **represents in some way human life.**

6. The outward offering of this visible gift signifies the inward offering or consecration of human life to

God—the giving to God of **"our whole heart."**

7. For a sacrifice three things are required—a **gift,** an **altar,** and a **priest.**

8. The Jewish people, taught by God Himself to offer sacrifice, frequently sacrificed animals (victims). The animal was slain and its blood poured out at the altar to express **three things:** (a) the gift or consecration of the people's lives to God, (b) repentance for sin and the wish to expiate it, (c) faith in a Redeemer to come, who would save us by His blood poured out in sacrifice for love of us.

"WEAK AND BEGGARLY ELEMENTS"

Although the Jewish sacrifices were prescribed by God, they were, as St. Paul tells us, but "weak and beggarly elements," for they had no power of themselves to appease God or cleanse souls from sin. They were only shadows or types or figures of the great Sacrifice to be offered by Jesus Christ, God the Son made man, "the Word made flesh."

In our chat on Original Sin and Redemption, my dear convert, I told you briefly of the great Sacrifice offered for us by Jesus Christ on Calvary. In our next chat I shall tell you about the great Sacrifice which He still offers on the altars of His Church—the Sacrifice of the Mass.

CHAPTER XX.

THE SACRIFICE OF THE MASS

BY uniting to Himself our passible, mortal nature in the Incarnation God the Son, the second Person of the Blessed Trinity, became both the Priest of the whole human race and its supreme Victim—the "one mediator between God and man." By offering Himself on Calvary He made infinite satisfaction for all human offences against God and bought at an infinite price all grace for mankind. The sacrifice of Redemption—the great sacrifice of Atonement—was more than sufficient to redeem mankind, and to its value nothing can be added. Non-Catholics, who state that the doctrine of the Mass diminishes or takes away from the all-sufficiency of Calvary, fail to grasp Catholic teaching, which most emphatically declares that, since the Sacrifice of Calvary is of infinite value and alone accomplished the redemption of mankind, no possible sacrifice could add to its inexhaustible store of satisfaction and merit. The Church teaches that the Mass is a relative, a sacramental, an unbloody sacrifice which sacramentally continues and renews the Sacrifice of the Cross by **representing, commemorating,** and **applying** Calvary.

CALVARY CONTINUED AND RENEWED

Our loving Savior wished to bring the great Sacrifice of Redemption down through every age to every soul, so that its saving waters might be applied until the end of the world to the sin-stained, parched souls of men in their strivings after life eternal. Calvary is like a measureless lake on the summit of an immense tableland, while the Mass is, as it were, a divine reservoir at the foot of the tableland, accessible to every weary traveller and conveying to him the heavenly waters of Calvary. Not only does the doctrine of the Mass not derogate or take away from the Sacrifice of Calvary, but, on the contrary, it emphasizes the infinitude, the beauty, and the necessity of that Sacrifice, which it brings vividly before us day by day.

The Mass **perpetuates** or renders perennial the Sacrifice of the Cross. It is **substantially the same sacrifice.** It is Calvary in sacramental garb. It is Calvary continued and renewed in a sacramental manner. I must explain this.

In the Mass there is the **same High Priest,** Jesus Christ, as on Calvary. We human priests are but His agents or instruments or mouthpieces, through whom He utters the same words of consecration as at the Last Supper and again changes bread and wine into His own body and blood. We are ordained priests to fulfil His own command: "Do this in commemoration, in remembrance, in memory of Me. Do what I have just done. Take bread and wine, utter over them the words I have said, and they will be changed into my body and blood, which I have just offered in sacramental sacrifice, and which I shall offer to-morrow for the redemption of man by my death." That is a paraphrase of Christ's words, or, if you wish, an amplification of them in their true meaning.

In the Mass there is the **very same Victim** as on Calvary—the Lamb of God. But Christ was victimized or immolated on Calvary by the real shedding of His blood, by the actual separation of His body and blood, which separation caused His death. Now, as St. Paul says, "Christ, rising from the dead, dieth no more; death hath no dominion over Him." Therefore He cannot again be victimized (made a victim) by the real shedding of His blood, by the real separation of His body and blood, by actual death. During His mortal life He could die and did die; His body and blood were separated in reality, and His soul actually left His body, although His Divinity (His divine nature) was inseparable from His human nature, from His soul and His body and blood. But since His glorious Resurrection His body and blood are actually inseparable, and His soul is inseparable from both. That is why, even though we receive Holy Communion under only one kind—in the form of either bread or wine—we receive the whole Christ, body, blood, soul and Divinity.

HOW CHRIST IS IMMOLATED AT MASS

How, then, does Christ become a victim at Mass? How is He immolated or victimized in this sacramental sacrifice? The answer is that He victimizes or immolates Himself in the Mass by putting Himself in the sacramental image of His real death on Calvary. This is done by the separate consecration of the bread and wine—by the distinct words: "This is my body; this is my blood." And these two sentences are uttered over two distinct species—bread and wine. Thus the body and blood of Christ are sacramentally separated by the words of consecration, and Christ, by thus putting Himself in the sacramental image of His death on the Cross, clearly shows that He is renewing the offering He made on the Cross, that He is again our victim, though in a different manner, that He is offering Himself in the unbloody sacrifice of the Mass in order to apply the fruits of the bloody sacrifice of the Cross, the Sacrifice of Redemption. Calvary is called the bloody sacrifice, the Mass the unbloody sacrifice, because on the Cross Christ actually shed His precious Blood and died, whereas in the Mass He does not really shed His blood, but only sacramentally.

SUMMARY OF THE CHURCH'S TEACHING

The Council of Trent—a great meeting of all the Bishops of the Church, assembled in the sixteenth century to deal with the errors of the "Reformers"—solemnly and beautifully declared the traditional teaching of the Church regarding the Mass. Let me give you a brief summary:

1. In the Blessed Eucharist the body and blood of Christ are truly, really, and substantially present under the species or appearances or accidents of bread and wine.

2. Although Christ redeemed us by the one supreme sacrifice of Calvary, the bloody sacrifice, still He gave the Church an unbloody sacrifice in order to represent, commemorate, and apply the Sacrifice of Calvary.

3. The Mass is a true and proper sacrifice, which gives God praise, appeases or placates His offended Majesty, and brings to our souls the precious fruits of Calvary.

4. In the Mass we have the same Divine Victim as on Calvary, and the same High Priest, who now offers Himself through the ministry of the Church's priests.

5. On Calvary Christ was sacrificed in a bloody manner, but in the Mass He is sacrificed in an unbloody manner.

Of course, by dear friend, that is but a brief summary of the chief points of the Church's doctrine.

You will learn much more about the Holy Sacrifice of the Mass as you go on—as you live a Catholic life. A great missionary of the seventeenth century, St. Leonard of Port Maurice, wrote in a wonderful little book ("The Hidden Treasure") that the Mass is the sun of Christianity, the heart of the Catholic religion, the centre of all its rites, and the sum of all that is beautiful in the Church of God.

PROOFS THAT MASS IS A TRUE SACRIFICE

It will be well, my dear convert, to give you some clear proofs that the Holy Eucharist, as instituted by Christ, is a true sacrifice.

1. In the prophecy of Malachy (or Malachias), which Protestants admit as inspired, we read these remarkable words spoken by God through His prophet: "From the rising of the sun even to the going down, my name is great among the gentiles, and **in every place there is sacrifice and there is offered to my name a clean oblation.** For my name is great among the gentiles, saith the Lord of hosts" (I., 11). From the purpose and context of Malachy's utterance it is clear that he spoke of a true sacrifice, which evidently was not that of the Jewish people nor the Sacrifice of the Cross (which was a bloody oblation). He mentioned a **clean oblation** (an unbloody sacrifice), which would be offered **in every place**, and, indeed, **every day** ("from the rising to the setting of the sun"). Now, either that prophecy has not been fulfilled (which would render it false), or the Mass is a true sacrifice, for, apart from the Mass, no unbloody sacrifice or "clean oblation" is offered up every day throughout the world.

2. At the Last Supper Jesus said: "This is my body **which is given for you"** (St. Luke, xxii., 19).

The word used by St. Paul, who wrote in Greek, has even a stronger meaning than **given,** for it really means **broken:** "This is my body, which is broken for you" (1 Cor. xi., 24). Both St. Luke and St. Paul use the present tense, although our English New Testament translates St. Paul's verb into the future tense.

Jesus said: "This is my blood, **which is shed for you** (or many)." Our English translation gives the future tense. There is, however, no objection to using the future, for Our Lord's words may be paraphrased thus: "This is my body, which is now sacramentally given for you, but which will be given to-morrow in crucifixion for you. This is my blood, which is now sacramentally shed in this chalice for you, but which will be really shed to-morrow for the whole world."

Of course, the word **broken** (used by St. Paul) can apply only to Christ's body at the Last Supper (in the Sacrament), for it was not broken on Calvary. In the Mass it is **sacramentally broken,** that is, broken under the form of bread.

Now, my dear friend, the very words Christ used at the Last Supper concerning His body and blood show that He truly offered Himself in sacrifice, truly made Himself a victim in the Holy Eucharist. **A body given or broken for us, blood shed for us,** can refer only to sacrifice, only to a victim offered in sacrifice, and indeed, only to a victim offered in a sacrifice of propitiation—a sacrifice for sin.

CHAPTER XXI.

SACRIFICE OF THE MASS (continued)

FURTHER PROOFS THAT THE MASS IS A SACRIFICE

TOWARDS the close of our last chat, my dear friend, I began to give you some proofs of the Catholic doctrine that the Eucharist, as instituted by Jesus Christ, is a true sacrifice. I gave you one proof from the prophecy of Malachy and another from the words used by Christ in the very words of institution. Let me now add three more proofs from Sacred Scripture Thus I am giving five proofs from the inspired writings.

3. At the Last Supper Our Lord said: "This is my blood of the **new testament.**" We know that the words, "of the New Testament," refer to the blood in the chalice, (a) because Christ used the present tense ("which is shed"), and (b) because St. Luke expresses Our Lord's words thus: "This is the chalice, the new testament in my blood," and St. Paul writes: "This chalice is the new testament in my blood."

The three Evangelists (Matthew, Mark, and Luke) and St. Paul all express the same truth correctly, of course; but St. Luke and St. Paul express more clearly that the blood of Jesus, sacramentally shed and offered in the chalice at the Last Supper, sealed the New Testament. Let me explain this.

What is a **testament?** The word has here two meanings: (a) **covenant,** or agreement or contract made between two or more persons; (b) **legacy,** or something bequeathed or left to us by a person's last will, which property or gift we receive when the testator dies.

(a) Under the Old Law God made a covenant or agreement, through Moses, at the foot of Mount Sinai with His chosen people. We read of this in the Book of Exodus, XIX.-XXII. This covenant was **sealed by the blood of sacrifice.** When Moses had told the Israelites what blessings and gifts God had promised them, the Israelites slew calves as victims, and Moses, having read "the book of the covenant" to the people and got them to promise to keep their part of the contract or compact with God, "took the blood and sprinkled it upon the people (he had already poured half of it on the altar) and said: **"This is the blood of the covenant** (testament) which the Lord hath made with you."

ALTAR PRESUPPOSES SACRIFICE

Under the New Law God has given us far more precious gifts and much greater blessings than in the Old Law, which was but a shadow or figure of the New Law. Christ promised most wonderful gifts and blessings to us and asked great love and service in return. This is the new law, the **new covenant** or compact between God and man, the **New Testament.** And Christ sealed this compact or covenant with the blood of sacrifice—with His own Precious Blood. That is why He said at the Last Supper: "This is My blood of the New Testament."

If we contrast Exodus XXIV., 7 and 8, with Luke XXII., 20, we can see at once that any Jew listening to Christ's solemn words at the Last Supper would understand them to refer to a true sacrifice offered at that moment.

(b) The word **testament** means also **legacy**—something which is bequeathed to us by a dying person, and which we receive when he dies. At the Last Supper, which Jesus celebrated just before His death, He bequeathed to us His body and blood in the Sacrifice of the Mass, together with all the gifts of Redemption. There also is the reason why He said: "This is my blood of the new testament."

Christ established and sanctioned (or sealed) the New Testament at the Last Supper by offering a sacramental sacrifice, and then solemnly confirmed that Testament by actually shedding His blood unto death on the next day (Good Friday).

4. St. Paul writes: "We have an **altar**, of which they have no power to eat who serve the tabernacle" (Hebrews XIII., 10). Those who "served the tabernacle" of the Old Testament were the adherents of the Jewish religion, which had now been abrogated, or, rather, fulfilled in the Christian religion. Only those who were baptized in Christ—who were fully Christians—could partake of the Divine Victim, the Lamb of God, immolated on the Christian altar. The word **altar** necessarily implies **sacrifice**. Without sacrifice there is no altar; where there is an altar sacrifice is offered. So, when St. Paul writes that we Christians have an altar and that only Christians may partake of it, he teaches that the Eucharist is a sacrifice.

5. In one of his Epistles to the Corinthians (I., Chap. X., 19-21) St. Paul writes of pagan sacrifices and warns us that we must not eat or drink the things pagans offer in sacrifice, and he calls the pagan altar "the table of devils." He speaks in the same passage of the Holy Eucharist, and it is quite clear from his contrast between "the chalice of the Lord" and "the chalice of devils," and between "the table of the Lord" and "the table of devils," that he regards the Eucharist as a true sacrifice. The whole passage, from verse 19

129

to verse 21, refers to sacrifice. Even the pagan Greeks, who offered sacrifice, called their altars sacred tables, or simply tables. We find the word table used in the Old Testament also for altar (Ezechiel XLIV., 16).

WHAT THE EARLY FATHERS SAY ABOUT THE MASS

In the writings of the early Fathers, whom I have already introduced to you, no doctrine is more clearly or emphatically taught than the truth that the Blessed Eucharist is a sacrifice. I shall give you but a few extracts from the writings of these great exponents of the Christian religion of the early centuries and you will see that the early Church taught and believed about the Mass exactly what we Catholics of to-day teach and believe.

1. The early Christians kept a faithful record of the lives and deaths of the martyrs. We find a clear expression of faith in the Eucharist as a sacrifice in the Acts of the martyrdom of St. Andrew, the Apostle. Even if these Acts were not written at the time of St. Andrew's death, they were certainly written not later than the third century, and are, therefore, an unmistakable testimony of the faith of the early Church.

The proconsul (a pagan Roman official) who was conducting the trial asked Andrew to offer sacrifice to the pagan gods, whereupon the Apostle replied: "Every day I immolate on the altar to God Almighty, who is one and true, not the flesh of bulls nor the blood of goats, but the spotless Lamb, and after all the faithful have eaten His flesh, the Lamb, who has been sacrificed, remains whole and living."

2. St. Irenaeus, of whom I have already spoken to you as being a most important witness to the faith of the early Church (both in the east and in the west), and who died in the year 202, wrote: "Christ acknowledged

the chalice of His blood and taught the new sacrifice of the New Testament, which the Church has received from the Apostles and offers to God throughout the world."

3. **St. Ambrose** (died 397): "If only an angel would stand at our side and render himself visible when we are burning incense at the altar, when we are offering the sacrifice! For you may not doubt that angels are present when Christ is there, when Christ is immolated."

4. **St. John Chrysostom** (+407): "When you see the Lord immolated and lying there, and the priest bending over the sacrifice, do you imagine yourself to be still among men and on this earth?"

5. **St. Cyril of Jerusalem** (+386): "When the spiritual sacrifice, the unbloody service, is completed, we pray to God over this sacrifice of propitiation for the universal peace of the churches, for the proper guidance of the world, for the emperor, soldiers, and companions, for the infirm and the sick, for those who are stricken with trouble, and in general for all who are in need of help we pray and offer up this sacrifice. We then commemorate the patriarchs, prophets, apostles, and martyrs, that God may, through their prayers and intercession, graciously accept our supplication. For all amongst us who have already departed this life we pray, since we believe that it will be of the greatest benefit to them if, in the presence of this holy and tremendous sacrifice, we make our petitions for them. The Christ, who was slain for our sins, we offer to propitiate the merciful God for those who are gone before and for ourselves."

EARLY LITURGIES OF THE CHURCH

The public, official service or worship offered to

God by the Church is known as **Liturgy**. Various books, approved by the Church, contain this Liturgy. The chief are the **Missal**, the book used at Mass; the **Ritual**, the book used in administering the sacraments and in imparting the Church's blessing to persons, places, and things; and the **Pontifical**, the book used by a Bishop in ordaining, confirming, and giving solemn blessings. Liturgical books were composed and used by the Church from the earliest times. Some of these books are called Sacramentaries.

Now, my dear friend, we find, when we study the early books of Liturgy used by the Church in various countries, that the Liturgy of the Mass always speaks of the Holy Eucharist as a sacrifice. In the ceremonies and prayers of these early Liturgies we read the words **offer, immolate, sacrifice, oblation, victim, unbloody sacrifice.** I could give you many extracts, but I shall close this chat with just a few.

1. **Liturgy of St. James:** "Let all mortal flesh be silent, standing there in fear and trembling; let all things of earth vanish from our thoughts. For the King of kings, the Lord of lords, Christ our God, is about to be sacrificed and given as food to the faithful. Before Him choirs of angels go, clothed with power and dominion, with faces veiled, chanting the hymn, Alleluia."

2. **Liturgy of St. John Chrysostom:** "Thou hast given us Thy only-begotten Son, the debtor and the debt, the victim and the Anointed, the Lamb and the Heavenly Bread, the High Priest and the Sacrifice, because He is always distributed amongst us without being consumed."

3. **Coptic Liturgy of St. Cyril:** "Make us worthy, O Lord, to present to Thee this holy, reasonable, spiritual

and unbloody sacrifice for the remission of our sins and for the pardon of the faults of the people."

4. **A prayer used in all the Churches of the East:—** The great Greek Doctor, St. Basil, who died in the year 379, wrote a letter to the clergy of Neo-Caesarea, in which he stated that the following prayer was recited in all the churches of the east: "Strengthen me, Almighty God, with the power of Thy Holy Spirit, and grant that I, clothed with the grace of the priesthood, may present myself at Thy holy table to offer to Thee Thy holy and immaculate Body and Thy precious Blood. I humbly beseech Thee not to turn Thy face from me, but graciously permit these gifts to be offered to Thee by Thy unworthy servant and sinner, as I am. For it is Thou who offerest and art offered; it is Thou who acceptest this sacrifice and who art distributed."

CHAPTER XXII.

THE CEREMONIES OF THE MASS

THE word **ceremony** is heard fairly often in ordinary conversation. "That man stands on ceremony." "Please avoid ceremony." "Who was M.C. (Master of Ceremonies) at the function?"

When we use this word, we are not necessarily speaking of anything religious. If a man lived like Robinson Crusoe, he would not have to bother about the rules of politeness—the way in which he should conduct himself at a concert or a dinner or a dance, the kind of suit he should wear at a Government House party, how he should address the King, etc.

But we all live in **society**, and therefore we have to follow certain rules or **conventions** in our relations or social intercourse with others. Such rules tell us, e.g., how we should address the King or the Governor-General; what kind of suits or frocks should be worn at certain functions; in what circumstances we should stand or sit or bow or raise our hat or remove it altogether. All these things—using special titles or forms of address, wearing certain kinds of clothes, standing, sitting, bowing, raising one's hat, uncovering one's head, etc.—are **social ceremonies**.

One who would pay no attention to such conventions would be called a boor. Just imagine a man entering a drawing-room without knocking, then standing with muddy, unwiped boots on the lovely carpet, looking around or staring at the invited ladies and gentlemen, keeping his hat on and his hands in his pockets, and lastly, without any introduction, bawling out: "Well, men and women, you ain't bad lookers. 'Ow's everythin'?"

NO MANNERS WITH GOD

Yet there are some people, my dear convert, who, while rightly adopting and strictly following social ceremonies, stupidly and foolishly say that we should not bother about ceremonies in our relations with God, in our solemn worship of our Creator. They imply, that is, that we should have manners towards creatures, but no manners towards the Creator. Of course, in practice, these people really do have some ceremonies, for it is practically impossible to do away with all ceremonies in religion. I have known certain non-Catholics to smile at Catholic ceremonies, as something silly or superstitious, and yet, when praying, to fall on one knee, bow their head, close their eyes, and rest their head on their hand. Why, what is all this but adopting ceremonies in order to show their reverence for God? And, if they admit some ceremonies (if they admit, that is, the principle underlying ceremonies), they cannot blame, but should rather praise, Catholics for surrounding the Holy Sacrifice of the Mass with all kinds of beautiful ceremonies.

Just imagine abolishing all ceremonies associated with this tremendous Sacrifice. Picture an ordinary rough table without a cloth, the priest standing there without a coat or collar, an ordinary pannikin (instead of a chalice), and all the people sitting around, the men wearing hats, and no one kneeling even at the consecration! Well, that is what cutting out all ceremonies would mean.

But, my dear friend, how different is the Mass with its splendid ceremonies! A beautiful altar (often adorned with flowers), a lovely gold or silver chalice, lighted wax candles, the priest robed in rich vestments, the people kneeling in awe and love at the consecration, and the priest genuflecting in adoration before the Blessed Sacrament!

GOD WISHES US TO HAVE CEREMONIES

If those people who object to the ceremonies of the Mass would only read the Bible, about which they talk so much, they would soon find out that God wishes ceremonies, that He positively commanded them to His chosen people in the Old Testament. In the Old Law God ordered many elaborate ceremonies, especially in regard to the sacrifices the Jewish priests offered. He explicitly commanded the use of vestments and even designated the vestments which His priests were to wear. You will find a full account of this in the Book of Exodus (XXV.-XXX.).

If it was fitting, and even prescribed by God, that priests in the Old Law should wear vestments while they offered to God sacrifices that were but "weak and beggarly elements" (as St. Paul calls such sacrifices), it is surely proper to surround with splendid ceremonies the great Sacrifice of the New Testament. Still, Christ did not positively prescribe vestments, but left that matter to His Church, which He empowered to make laws regarding that and other matters when He said to Peter: "Whosoever thou shalt bind on earth, it shall be bound also in heaven." Christ instituted the wonderful Sacrifice of the New Law, consecrated His Apostles priests, and left to the Church the ordering of the accidental ceremonies that should surround its celebration. I say **accidental** ceremonies, for the Church has no power over the **substance** or **essence** of the Sacrifice of the Mass, which consists in changing bread and wine into the body and blood of Christ, who thereby offers Himself, through the ministry of His priests, in order to represent, commemorate, and apply the Sacrifice of Redemption. But the Church can designate what vestments the priest is to wear, in what language Mass is to be offered, what ceremonies are to surround its celebration, in what place and at what hour the Holy Sacrifice should be celebrated, etc.

DEVELOPMENT OF CHRISTIAN CEREMONIAL

In the early centuries, when Christians, owing to fierce persecution, had to assemble in secret often down in the catacombs (underground cemeteries), to offer Mass, they could not, of course, have the magnificent churches and the grand ceremonial which they began to enjoy when the Church, during the reign of Constantine, converted to Christianity, was granted freedom. But even in those dark days, assembled in secret, Christians surrounded the celebration of the Eucharistic Sacrifice with what splendor they could.

In the beginning priests, in offering Mass, wore the best and neatest civilian garb of the time, and, as vesture changed with the times, the Church, always conservative in her religious practices, retained that ancient garb, which accordingly became religious vestments. An altar was always, of course, used for the Sacrifice. In the catacombs it was a slab of marble placed above a martyr's tomb, and, when the Church emerged from the catacombs, she retained the touching practice of using at least an altar-stone (even though the larger altar was of wood) in which were inserted relics of martyrs or saints. You will find that beautiful custom still in vogue. Later on, my dear friend, I shall tell you of the honor which we rightly pay to the relics of saints. Candles were used in the catacombs and in other secret places in order to give light during the Holy Sacrifice, and the Church retains the use of candles because of their symbolic meaning, which I shall presently explain.

VESTMENTS, CANDLES, BELL

Something connected with divine worship may have had a natural, necessary origin and yet be retained because of its mystical or symbolic significance. Thus originally the book was transferred from one side of the altar to the other in order to make room for the offerings of the congregation—bread and wine—which were laid upon the altar. But the practice of moving the Missal (Mass-book) has been retained in order to symbolize or remind us that, when the Jews rejected the teaching of Christ, His Gospel was carried to the Gentiles by the Apostles.

The vestments used at Mass have also a symbolic meaning: they bring to our mind the Passion of Our Saviour by symbolizing the cloth with which He was blindfolded, the cords with which He was bound to the pillar, the purple robe with which He was clothed, and the cross which He carried. The prayers, too, which the priest recites while vesting for Mass, show that the Church attaches a beautiful spiritual significance to each vestment.

The lighted candles symbolize Him who said: "I am the light of the world." And they remind us of His words: "So let your light shine before men, that they may see your good works and glorify your Father who is in heaven."

The bell is rung to announce to the people—often a large congregation in a spacious church—the most important parts of the Mass, for some of the congregation may be so far from the altar as to be unable to hear, or even see, the priest, and the sound of the sanctuary bell tells them exactly when each important part of the Holy Sacrifice is taking place.

WHY MASS IS SAID IN LATIN

Mass is said in Latin, but the laity are not asked to pray in Latin. All your prayers, my dear convert, at home and in the Church, will be said in English, and, when the priest prays with the people, he uses English—or, I should say, the language which the people speak. But the Mass is not a mere form of prayer —it is a **sacrifice**; it is a **sacred action**. The people all know that the tremendous sacrifice is being offered, and they join with the priest in offering the Divine Victim. Mass could, of course, be said in any language, and, indeed, in the Universal Church we find the same sacrifice celebrated in several languages. But Latin is used most widely. Latin is a dead, unchanging language, and it is fitting that the unchanging Sacrifice should be offered in an unchanging language, as it is offered even in those countries that do not use Latin. Besides, it is fitting that the Universal Church—the Catholic Church—should have a universal or Catholic language and that, for the sake of greater unity, such a language should be very widely used—in countries that differ in their own language from one another. But you, my dear friend, will use your own language in your prayers at Mass. Many of our laity fittingly use a Missal or Mass-book, which contains the very same prayers which the priest is reciting, though such prayers are translated, for the benefit of the laity, into the vernacular (their own language).

And now, my dear convert, I have given you many chats on the Mass, because the Eucharistic Sacrifice is the very center of Catholic worship. You will learn more about this marvelous gift of Divine Love as you go on in the Church. The Mass is an inexhaustible treasure, and I hope that, when you become a Catholic, all your life will center around this "clean oblation" which, as the Prophet Malachy, enlightened by God, foretold, is now offered up throughout the nations "from the rising of the sun to the going down."

CHAPTER XXIII.

THE PRIEST'S POWER OF FORGIVENESS

NOTE: I should like to give a special chat on Holy Communion, but as I have already devoted six chats to the Blessed Eucharist, I shall now pass on to the Sacrament of Penance. Besides, from what has been said on the Real Presence and the Mass, it will be easy for the instructor to add a talk that will prepare the convert for first Holy Communion. Several of my own converts this year have assured me that they derived great help, in preparing for First Communion, from the pamphlet, "Talks With Little Children," published by the Paulist Press, N. Y. C. Even as I type this note a young man, whom I am to receive into the Church to-morrow, is reading that pamphlet with great interest and he states that it is most helpful. Another man, whom I received into the Church two months ago, declared that this simple pamphlet helped him considerably at this stage of his instructions. Therefore I recommend instructors of converts to procure this booklet and to get their converts to use it immediately before their reception of First Communion.

WHAT IS CONFESSION?

Penance is the sacrament by which sins committed after Baptism are forgiven. The Catholic Church teaches that Christ gave power to His Apostles to forgive sin, that this power passed on to the Bishops and priests of the Church, and that, in order to get this forgiveness, the sinner must make known his sins to the priest in confession.

Some persons outside the Church have a very hazy notion, others a very queer notion, of what is meant by confession. Some say that Catholics must pay to get absolution (forgiveness from the priest), whereas the truth is that, even if a sinner offered a priest a million pounds for absolution, the priest could not grant it unless the sinner were rightly disposed; and that, even if a penitent were a beggarman, the priest would be obliged to give him absolution if he were rightly disposed. Other persons say that, as long as Catholics tell their sins to the priest, they may go on committing whatever sins they wish, whereas the truth is that, unless a sinner is truly sorry for his sins and is determined, with God's grace, not to commit them again, his confession would be worse than useless.

Confession means that the sinner kneels before the priest and with a humble and contrite heart declares all his sins—at least all the grievous sins which burden his soul. By the sinner I mean every member of the Church who has attained the use of reason—everyone from the Pope himself down to the lowliest schoolchild, for we are all sinners, and only Mary, the Mother of Christ, of whom I shall speak in another chat, was absolutely free from sin, original and actual, a privilege conferred on her through the merits of her Divine Son, Who is Holiness Incarnate.

The priest hears the confession under the most inviolable secrecy. Under no circumstances whatever may a priest make known a single sin, however small it may appear, that was told in Confession by some particular person. Cases are on record of priests who have cheerfully submitted to imprisonment and death rather than violate the sacred seal of Confession.

When the Confession is finished, the priest addresses words of sympathy, of advice, and of encouragement, and, if satisfied that the penitent is truly sorry for his sins and has a firm purpose of avoiding, with God's help, future sin, he pronounces, in God's name, over the repentant soul the sentence of forgiveness. The penitent then departs, confident that now he has regained God's friendship, experiencing in his soul that "peace which surpasseth all understanding."

BEAUTY OF CONFESSION

The practice I have outlined must appeal to every right-thinking person, even though he does not believe in the divinity of its institution. It is natural to every human heart to unburden itself to a faithful friend in time of distress or sorrow. Bacon, the English writer, in a beautiful essay on friendship, shows how, when we confide in a friend in time of sorrow or trouble, half our trouble is borne by our friend. And surely, when our soul is weighed down or crushed under the burden of sin, it is sweet and helpful to disclose our trouble to a friend who will sympathize with us and keep our secret. I could mention cases of non-Catholics, of some persons who had no religion, coming to a priest in order to make known in confidence their moral failings and to seek comfort and advice. This shows that there is a natural instinct urging us to make quiet, secret confession of some kind. That natural instinct Christ has raised to a supernatural level by instituting sacramental confession. The Catholic recognizes in confession something far more than a mere confidential disclosure of his sins in order to find some solace. In the priest he recognizes one who, although human like himself, has received power to forgive sin.

AN OBJECTION REFUTED

The following objection is often raised by our non-Catholic friends: "You Catholics ascribe to a mere man a power that belongs to God alone. No one but God can forgive sin. How can any man possibly do so? To attempt to do so is to arrogate to one's self a divine attribute. The idea is preposterous."

To any Protestant who raises such an objection we need simply reply: "But my dear friend, you also ascribe to mere men powers that belong to God alone, for, in accepting the incidents recorded in the Bible, as you rightly do, you admit that, both in the Old and in the New Testament, mere men—Moses, the prophets, and the apostles—worked miracles, even raised the dead to life. Now, only God can work miracles such as some of the wonders performed by those men; only God can raise the dead to life."

The answer to these difficulties is that certainly God alone, by His Own Power, can forgive sin or perform the highest miracles, but He can, if He wishes, exercise those powers through a human agency. A certain distinguished Anglican convert once remarked that God could, if He chose to do so, forgive sin through stones!

The point to prove is not whether God can delegate or depute men to forgive sins, but whether He actually has done so.

CHRIST GAVE THE APOSTLES POWER TO FORGIVE SIN

Our Lord first promised His Apostles power to forgive sin. We read of this solemn promise in the Gospel of St. Matthew (XVIII., 18): "Amen, I say to you, whatsoever you shall bind on earth shall be bound also in heaven; and whatsoever you shall loose on earth shall be loosed also in heaven."

By these words Christ promised the Apostles great power—power to make laws for the Church (the power of binding), power to dispense from laws (the power of loosing), and power to forgive sins (the power of loosing). It is especially the power of loosing which concerns us in the present chat. Obviously the object of this power was not an ox or a horse; no special power is required to untie or loose an animal. The work of the Apostles was to save the souls of men, and therefore the power of loosing, here solemnly promised to them, must have referred to human souls. Now sin is the chain or fetter that enthrals the human soul, that prevents it from rising to God. While the soul is enslaved by the fetters of sin, it cannot be united to God; if those chains are coiled around it when it passes into eternity, it will remain separated from God forever. But the Apostles, whose ministry was to save souls, were promised power to burst asunder those fetters of sin, power to forgive sin: "Whatsoever you shall loose on earth shall be loosed also in heaven." Remark, too, that the sentence in heaven follows the sentence pronounced by the Apostles on earth.

This solemn promise Our Savior fulfilled on the day of His glorious resurrection. On the very day on which He rose from the dead He gave the Apostles power to raise souls from the death of sin. On the very day on which He rose to a glorious life He gave the Apostles power to raise sin-laden souls to the life of grace. On the very day of His own glorious Resurrection He gave the Apostles power to confer on sinful souls a spiritual resurrection. St. John records the conferring of this great power on the Apostles. Consider Christ's words as recorded by the unerring pen of the inspired Evangelist:

"He said therefore to them again: Peace be to you.

As the Father hath sent Me, I also send you. When He said this, He breathed on them and said to them: Receive ye the Holy Ghost. Whose sins you shall forgive, they are forgiven them; and whose sins you shall retain, they are retained" (XX., 21-23).

CHRIST'S WORDS CLEAR

We may paraphrase Our Lord's words thus: "As the Father has sent Me, I send you. As My Father has sent Me into this world to reconcile sinners with God, so, now that I am returning to the Father, I send you, my ambassadors, out into the world to carry on the work of forgiveness which it has been my delight to exercise for the past three years. But, if you are to continue my work of mercy and forgiveness, you will need a participation in My power, and this I now give you, as I have already promised it to you. Receive the Holy Ghost. Whose sins you forgive are forgiven, and whose sins you retain are retained."

Note, my dear friend, that the sentence of God follows the sentence of forgiveness. God's forgiveness follows the Apostles' forgiveness; God's withholding of forgiveness (retaining) follows the Apostles' retaining of sin. The words of Christ are so clear, that it is passing strange that any Christian who reads his Bible can fail to see that Our Lord actually gave the Apostles the power to forgive sin.

CHAPTER XXIV.

CONFESSION

IN our last chat, my dear convert, I showed you that Christ gave power to the Apostles to forgive sin. To any Christian who admits that truth it should be clear that this power did not cease with the death of the Apostles, but was passed on by them to successors and will remain in the Church for ever. But, since we do meet persons who question the continuance of this power in the Church, although they may be ready to admit that it was conferred on the Apostles (a rather silly attitude, to say the least), I shall briefly deal with this matter.

THE POWER OF FORGIVENESS REMAINS IN THE CHURCH

Since the Church will remain till the end of time as Christ instituted it (as I explained in our chats about the Church), so the powers Our Lord gave the Apostles for the actual saving (and sanctifying) of souls **must always continue** in the Church. Otherwise the Church would change, and this it cannot do. Besides, souls will have to be saved until the end, and so they will need the helps Christ left His Church for that purpose. For example, Baptism will always have to be administered, for all children of Adam (except Mary Immaculate) come into this world with original sin on their souls, for they were conceived with it, and Baptism is the Sacrament Our Savior instituted to blot out that stain and make us adopted children of God. Hence Baptism was intended by Christ not merely for the ages of the Apostles, but for all time.

Again, Christ's command to receive His body and blood holds always. But, unless the power which the Apostles received to change bread and wine into the body and blood of Christ was passed on, how are we to obey Our Lord's precept?

Likewise, the power of forgiveness is needed at all times. There will be sinners till the end of the world, and they will require forgiveness. Therefore **Jesus must have meant the power of forgiveness to continue in His Church.**

We might put this in another way: Christ founded a Church to last unchanged to the end of the world. He gave that Church authority and power to teach, rule, and sanctify men. That authority and power, therefore, will ever remain in the Church.

WHY CONFESS SINS TO A PRIEST

To obtain pardon of our sins we must go to confession—that is, we must tell the priest all mortal sins we have committed since our last good confession, or, if one is making his first confession, all the mortal sins he has committed since Baptism. We need not tell venial sins in confession, though it is praiseworthy to do so. You will learn in due time all about sin and its distinctions. Mortal sin is a grievous sin—one which destroys our friendship with God and deserves everlasting punishment. Venial sin is a lesser offence against God—one of those faults into which even just souls may fall.

A little Catholic girl was once asked by a non-Catholic companion why Catholics went to confession to a priest. The Catholic child is reported to have given this simple beautiful answer: "When Jesus was on this earth, He forgave people their sins. But He knew everyone's sins, because He is God. When He was leaving this earth, He gave His priests power to forgive sin. But the priest does not know the people's sins, and so they must tell them to him."

THE PRIEST IS A JUDGE

A judge has authority from the State to sentence persons guilty of crime or to acquit those who are accused and proved innocent. The judge (generally guided by a jury) has to decide first whether the accused person is guilty or innocent. Although he has authority from the State to condemn or acquit, he must first hear the evidence and form his opinion. It would be absurd for a judge to pronounce sentence without first hearing the case.

Now, the priest has been appointed to pronounce sentence in the name of Christ. He is a judge with delegated authority. He must **bind** (refuse forgiveness) or **loose** (grant forgiveness); he must **forgive** or **retain** (withhold forgiveness). These are the words Christ Himself used. Since the priest is a judge in this matter, he must first hear the case. But it is the sinner himself who gives evidence. The sinner in this tribunal is both the accused and the accuser. And, indeed, there are many circumstances which a priest should know before he can reasonably decide whether a sinner is disposed for forgiveness. Let me mention one or two. Suppose that a person had stolen a serious amount—the priest must ascertain whether such a person is willing to restore what he has sinfully taken. A man may be living with another man's wife—the priest must find out whether this sinner is willing to leave this woman. In a word, the priest must satisfy

his own conscience that the penitent is sincerely sorry.
This can be done ordinarily only through confession.

THE PRIEST ALSO A PHYSICIAN

The priest is also a physician appointed by Christ
to heal souls. Now, a patient must make known to a
doctor what his ailments are. He must submit to
medical examination if he wishes the doctor to cure
him. The Fathers of the Church applied this example
to sacramental confession. I shall quote St. John
Chrysostom on this matter soon. You will see how
the early Fathers of the Church required confession to
a priest. And you must remember that they had received their doctrine fresh from the Apostles.

CONFESSION MENTIONED IN THE BIBLE

Confession is mentioned in the Bible. I pass over
some texts in the Old Testament (which, of course, do
not refer to **sacramental** confession); I omit to dwell
on the fact that those who were baptized by St. John
the Baptist "confessed their sins"; I come to a striking
passage in the Epistle of St. James, in which, after
mentioning the sacrament of Extreme Unction (to
which I have already referred), the Apostle adds:
"Confess therefore your sins **to one another**" (or "one to
another"—V., 16).

From what precedes these words it is clear that
St. James is speaking of confession to "the priests of
the Church." But, for argument's sake, let us suppose that he is here referring to confession made to any
Christian. (Certainly no one can possibly see here any
allusion to confession to God!) We could then reason
thus: If, according to St. James, it is a good thing to
confess one's sins to anyone at all, with greater reason
do we Catholics make our confession to a priest, who,

as I have shown, has received power from Christ to forgive sin.

AN INDIRECT, THOUGH VERY CLEAR, PROOF

Let us now, my dear friend, take another simple proof which shows convincingly that Christ instituted sacramental confession. This argument may be stated in a simple manner: If Christ had not instituted auricular confession (confession to be made to a priest), then it never would have been instituted; but, since confession is in existence throughout the Catholic Church (and certain other Christian churches), undoubtedly it must be of divine origin. Before I give you certain striking passages from the early Fathers, which show that confession was believed in and practiced from the earliest ages of Christianity, let me expand the simple indirect argument I have mentioned.

I say that, apart from divine institution, it is evident that there would be no such thing as obligatory confession of sin to a priest. Why? Because neither the laity nor the clergy would have instituted such a practice. Not the laity, for they never would have imposed on themselves the difficult obligation of kneeling before a fellow man and disclosing to him even their most secret and most shameful sins.

Not the clergy—for two reasons. First, because the work of the confessional is the most trying part of a priest's ministry. There is nothing poetic or attractive about sitting for hours in a stuffy confessional, listening to penitent after penitent confessing sins. There is no natural inducement to go into a hospital of plague-stricken patients, at the risk of contracting the plague, in order to hear the confessions of dying persons. There is no romance in rising at dead of night and going out in inclement weather, often a great distance, in order to absolve a person who is dangerously ill. There is no natural attraction to go on a battle-field, at the risk of being blown to pieces, in order to give absolution to soldiers. Men do not do such things for a mere superstition, for some vain human invention. No, but every priest will gladly give his life rather than allow even one soul to pass into eternity without the grace of absolution, for he is most firmly convinced that the power of absolving and the obligation of confession come from Jesus Christ. Certainly the clergy would not have imposed on themselves the obligation of doing the things I have just now mentioned.

A second reason why the clergy would not have instituted confession is that this obligation falls on them just as on the laity. In the Catholic Church there is not one law for the clergy and another for the laity, except that the clergy are burdened with more laws than the laity. And the law of confession binds the clergy just as strictly as it obliges the laity. Priests, Bishops, Cardinals, even the Pope himself—all are bound to go to confession just like the lowliest school-child. No, the clergy would certainly not have imposed on themselves this difficult obligation.

Since neither laity nor clergy would have invented confession, it must be of divine institution.

Besides, if this practice were of human institution, surely history would not be silent regarding the origin of so important and difficult an obligation. What Pope, what General Council, instituted it? Of this history says not a word, for the simple reason that the Sacrament of Penance was not instituted by the Church, but came from God. And now, my dear friend, I shall give you some clear passages from the early Fathers of the Church to show that the Church ever taught confession as a divinely instituted practice.

WHAT THE EARLY FATHERS SAY OF CONFESSION

It will be well now, my dear friend, to consult the Fathers again, with whom you have become familiar. They are unassailable witnesses of the faith and practice of the early Church. I shall single out a few:

St. Cyprian (d. 258): "We find that no one ought to be forbidden to do penance and that to those who implore the mercy of God peace can be granted through His priests. . . . Because in hell there is no confession . . . those who repent with their whole heart and ask for it should be received into the Church and therein saved unto the Lord."

St. Pacian, Bishop of Barcelona (d. 390): "This (forgiving sins), you say, only God can do. Quite true; but what He does through His priests is the exercise of His own power."

St. Ambrose (d. 397): "The Church obeys Him (the Lord) in both respects, by binding sin and by loosing it; for the Lord willed that for both the power should be equal. . . . It seemed impossible that sins should be forgiven through penance; Christ granted this (power) to the Apostles, and from the Apostles it has been transmitted to the office of priests."

St. John Chrysostom (d. 407): "As often as you sin, come to me, and I shall heal you. . . . Be not ashamed to approach (the priest) because you have sinned; nay, rather, for this very reason approach. No one says: Because I have an ulcer, I will not go near a physician or take medicine; on the contrary, it is just this that makes it needful to call in physicians and apply remedies. We (priests) know well how to pardon, because we ourselves are liable to sin."

St. Athanasius (d. 373): "As the man whom the

priest baptizes is enlightened by the grace of the Holy Ghost, so does he who in penance confesses his sins receive through the priest forgiveness in virtue of the grace of Christ."

St. Augustine (d. 430): "Let us not listen to those who say that the Church has not power to forgive sins."

St. Leo I. (reigned as Pope 440-461): "It is sufficient that the guilt of consciences be made known to priests alone by secret confession." (Yet he recommended or praised public confession.)

In 452 this great Pope wrote thus to a bishop named Theodore: "The pardon of God can be obtained only by the prayers of priests. . . . For the Mediator between God and man, the man Christ Jesus (I. Tim. II., 5) gave this power to the prelates of the Church, that they can give the action of penance to those who confess, and can admit these same persons, purified by salutary satisfaction, to the participation of the sacraments, through the door of reconciliation."

CHAPTER XXV.

INDULGENCES

THE Catholic teaching regarding Indulgences is greatly misunderstood and often misrepresented. One reason is that the English word **indulgence**, in its ordinary meaning, does not express the strict meaning of the Latin from which it is derived. The Latin word, **indulgentia** really means **forgiveness** or **remission.** Some non-Catholics seem to think that by an indulgence Catholics mean permission to commit sin. The truth is that an indulgence is not even forgiveness of sin itself, but merely the remission of the temporal punishment which often remains after the guilt of sin has been forgiven.

A SIMPLE ILLUSTRATION

To bring home to your mind, my dear friend, the real meaning of an indulgence, let me give you an easy illustration in the form of a story. A little boy named Tom once disobeyed his father, and as a punishment the father said that Tom, who loved a game of football, was not to play that game for a whole month. After a fortnight, during which time the little boy sorrowfully underwent his penance, his sister, Betty, a lovely child whom her father worshipped, took pity on her brother and begged her dad to let Tom off the remainder of his punishment. The father replied: "Very well, Betty, if Tom washes the dishes to-day instead of letting you do so, I shall let him off the remaining fortnight of his punishment." Tom gladly washed the dishes and then went out happily to play football. In this case one act of washing dishes—an easy matter—gained for Tom **an indulgence of fourteen days.** For washing the dishes once the lad's father **remitted** a whole fortnight of punishment or penance; the father, in other words, commuted a fortnight's difficult penance into a simple action which cost little effort. I shall return to this example presently.

CATHOLIC TEACHING STRICTER THAN PROTESTANT REGARDING SIN

The true doctrine of indulgences shows that the Catholic Church has a stricter teaching about sin than Protestants have. Non-Catholics say that, when God forgives sin, there is no longer any debt due to His Majesty, so that, if a person died immediately after getting forgiveness of any sins whatever, the soul of that person would go immediately to heaven. The Catholic Church, however, teaches that, when God forgives sin, He often requires some **expiation** of that forgiven sin. He exacts a **temporal** punishment for it, so that, ordinarily, such a soul, if it passed into eternity before it had undergone such punishment or expiation, would have to pass some time in **Purgatory** before being admitted into heaven. I shall have a special chat with you about purgatory soon.

The sacrament of Baptism blots out not only all guilt or stain of sin, but also all punishment due to sin. Hence a soul which passed to judgment immediately after baptism would be admitted at once to the eternal vision of God. But when sins committed after Baptism are forgiven either in the Sacrament of Penance or because a sinner has made an act of perfect sorrow (perfect contrition) with the intention of going to confession in due time, generally some debt of temporal punishment still remains due to God's offended Majesty.

THE CHURCH HAS POWER TO GRANT INDULGENCES

Christ gave the Church power to forgive sin and also to remit this temporal punishment His words to Peter are unrestricted—He promised Peter power to loose whatever he saw fit to loose on earth: "Whatsoever thou shalt loose on earth it shall be loosed also in heaven" (Matt. XVI., 18). This power He later promised to all the Apostles, in union with Peter (XVIII., 18). Thus, as the Church has received from her Divine Founder the power of forgiving sin, so has she received from Him the power to remit the temporal punishment due to forgiven sin. "The greater includes the less."

Forgiveness of sin means that the **guilt** of sin and the **eternal punishment** due to mortal or grievous sin are cancelled, but it does not mean that the **temporal punishment** or expiation due is necessarily remitted. Generally speaking, this debt is not remitted.

CANONICAL PENANCES IN THE EARLY CHURCH

In the early ages the Church used to impose long, severe penances for sins told in confession. They are called "canonical penances." Here are some examples of these severe penances: long fasts (sometimes extending over years); standing outside the church during Mass; hard pilgrimages—journeys to sacred spots in trying circumstances; lying prostrate on the ground; giving alms—money or other gifts—to the poor.

At times, because a prospective martyr (one who was in prison and under sentence of death for the faith) or a confessor (one who had bravely suffered

for the faith) **interceded** for a sinner who had to undergo a long period of penance (as Betty in our little
story interceded for Tom), the Church remitted the
remainder of a long, hard penance; that is, she granted
the sinner an **indulgence.**

When the Church now grants an indulgence of
seven years or of three hundred days to those who say
a certain prayer or perform a certain exercise of devotion, this does not mean, as some people think, seven
years or three hundred days off our time in purgatory;
no, it simply means that for such a prayer or such an
act the Church remits as much of the temporal punishment due to forgiven sin as seven years or three
hundred days of those severe canonical penances in the
early centuries would have cancelled. In other words,
an indulgence is simply a **commutation** of one good
work into another, a substitution of something easier
for something more difficult, the easier work being
assigned by the Church's authority the same efficacy of
satisfying or cancelling temporal punishment as the
more difficult work. Tom's washing the dishes was
much easier for him than abstinence from football
for a fortnight; yet his father attached to it the same
efficacy or accepted it as if it had the same satisfactory
value.

An indulgence of seven years or three hundred
days is known as a **partial** indulgence, for it remits
part of the punishment due to forgiven sin (though, of
course, for some persons this **could** be a full remission,
as they might not owe God's justice much expiation).
At times the Church attaches to some good work or
prayer a **plenary** indulgence, which means complete
or full remission of the temporal punishment due to
forgiven sin.

INDULGENCES TAUGHT IN SCRIPTURE AND TRADITION

Thus you see, my dear convert, that the Catholic doctrine of indulgences shows that we have a stricter notion than non-Catholics of sin and the debt due to God's offended Majesty. You see also that the doctrine flows from Christ's clear words to Peter, the first Pope. I might add, too, that we read in the New Testament that St. Paul granted an indulgence to the incestuous Corinthian (2 Corinthians II., 10, compared with 1 Cor. V., 3-5). And you now realize that the practice has ever been in vogue in the Church, as it still is, of granting partial or complete remission of the temporal punishment or expiation which generally remains after the sin itself has been forgiven.

CHAPTER XXVI.

THE SACRAMENT OF MATRIMONY

I HAVE already explained to you, my dear friend, the sacraments in general—the meaning of a sacrament, the number of the sacraments, and the name of each. I have given you detailed explanations of the Blessed Eucharist and Penance. It will be well, before closing the Chats about the Sacraments and passing on to another subject, to deal at length with the Sacrament of Matrimony and to explain in particular the Church's legislation known as the "Ne Temere" Decree, which is now embodied in the New Code of Canon Law (Ecclesiastical or Church Law) that was promulgated in 1918. (The "Ne Temere" Decree was the extension, in 1908, to the Universal Church of certain legislation that had been already in vogue in many countries since the sixteenth century.)

MARRIAGE AS A CONTRACT

By marriage (a simpler word with the same meaning as matrimony) two persons, a man and a woman, make a solemn contract (a serious or solemn agreement) whereby they promise or pledge that they will live together for the rest of their life as husband and wife, will be always faithful to each other, and will carry out the sacred duties of married life.

There are many contracts; of these you have experience in your daily life. When you buy an article, you make a contract with the seller to pay him a price and he enters a contract to hand over into your possession the object you purchase. Once you both agree to the terms of this contract and pledge yourselves to it, you are each bound in justice to keep your respective parts of the agreement. Other examples of contracts are borrowing, lending, letting, renting, hiring labor, undertaking to work for an employer, etc.

The contract known as matrimony or marriage is a very solemn contract, arising from the very law of nature, for the propagation of the human race. This contract existed from the beginning of the human race, and it is found amongst all peoples, even pagans.

MARRIAGE AS A SACRAMENT

But every marriage contract is not a sacrament. We may, and do, find many a matrimonial contract that is not a sacrament. True marriage exists among pagans, but pagans do not receive the **sacrament** of marriage. Even amongst God's chosen people in the Old Law (the Jewish people) marriage was not a sacrament. Christ raised the contract of matrimony to the level of a sacrament. When precisely He did so is not clear, but His infallible Church (about which you have already been well instructed) teaches as an article of faith that He did so. We read in the New Testament that, just before He entered on His public life, He and His Blessed Mother attended a wedding in Cana of Galilee. We read that, during His public life, He stressed the **unity** and **indissolubility** of marriage. By the unity of marriage is meant that a man may not have two wives simultaneously or a woman two husbands at the same time. Of course, if one married partner dies, then the living partner is free to enter another marriage. By the indissolubility of marriage we mean that the bond of marriage—the marriage tie

—cannot be dissolved while both partners live; we mean that **divorce** is contrary to the Christian teaching. "Every one that putteth away his wife, and marrieth another," declared Christ, "commiteth adultery; and he that marrieth her that is put away from her husband, commiteth adultery" (Luke XVI., 18).

St. Paul, in his inspired Epistle to the Ephesians, writes beautifully of marriage between Christians and implies that it is a true sacrament. I would ask you to read carefully the fifth chapter of this Epistle, verses 22-32, where you will see that the Apostle teaches that such a marriage is a sacred sign—a sign or symbol of Christ's union with the Church; that it is a sign of grace. And the Apostle implies that it actually produces grace. In fact, St. Paul explicitly calls such a marriage a **great sacrament,** though I do not maintain for certain that St. Paul is using the word **sacrament** in this sentence in the strict sense in which I defined the term in our chat about the Sacraments. Still, the whole tenor of this beautiful passage to which I refer in the Epistle to the Ephesians implies that marriage between Christians is a true sacrament. However, we know with certainty from **Tradition** (of which I have already explained the meaning), and especially from the Church's solemn teaching, that marriage between baptized persons is a true sacrament.

Thus we see that, although marriage is always a solemn contract, it is not always a sacrament. Unbaptized persons cannot receive any sacrament except, of course, Baptism. But between baptized persons the contract of marriage and the sacrament of matrimony are absolutely inseparable. If two baptized persons truly marry, then they must at the same time receive the sacrament of matrimony, for this sacrament is simply marriage between baptized persons; it is a **sacramental contract.**

THE CHURCH'S AUTHORITY OVER MARRIAGE

The State has authority over merely civil contracts. It may prescribe that, unless certain conditions are fulfilled, certain civil contracts which would otherwise be valid or binding will have no force whatever—that they will be **null and void.** Or the State may declare that, unless certain conditions are fulfilled, it will reserve the authority to **annul** such contracts, so that, after the pronouncement of a sentence of nullity by a competent judge, such contracts will no longer have any binding force. For instance, the State may require, for the validity of certain contracts, that they be made in writing, that the persons who make them sign their names to the document, and that two witnesses also sign their names in the presence of the contracting parties and in the presence of each other. No reasonable person questions the authority of the State to legislate thus in regard to certain civil contracts.

Now, as the State has such authority over merely civil contracts and exercises this authority for the common good of its citizens by legislation, so the Church has ever rightly claimed a similar authority over the sacramental contract of matrimony. The sacraments have been entrusted to the Church by her Divine Founder, who instituted them. And, since one of those sacraments is essentially a contract, the Church must have the same authority over that sacramental contract as the State has over ordinary civil contracts. That the Church has such authority is clear from Christ's words to Peter: "Whatsoever thou shalt bind on earth shall be bound also in heaven" (Matt. XVI., 19). And this authority the Church has always claimed and exercised.

IMPEDIMENTS OF MARRIAGE

An **impediment** to marriage is an **obstacle** which

the Church puts in the way of marriage, just as the State may "block" the validity of certain civil contracts. The latter contracts would be valid unless the State intervened, and many marriages would be valid unless the Church intervened. At times the Church forbids certain marriages without making them invalid, just as the State makes laws which declare certain contracts illegal, though not making them null and void. An impediment which renders a marriage invalid (or null and void) is called a **diriment** or **annulling** impediment, while an impediment which simply renders a marriage unlawful, while leaving it valid, is called a **prohibitory** impediment. For the moment I am concerned with annulling impediments.

A well-known instance of such impediment is **blood relationship**, technically termed **consanguinity**. According to the natural law marriage between first cousins or between second cousins would be a true marriage; but the Church, exercising her authority, has put an annulling impediment in the way of such marriages, so that now they would be null and void. Of course, the Church may, for a just reason, dispense from such an impediment, which means that she allows such a marriage in special circumstances—she suspends or relaxes her law in that particular case.

THE FAMOUS "NE TEMERE" DECREE

You have probably heard or read of the Church's law known as the "Ne Temere" Decree, which was promulgated in New Zealand and Australia in the year 1908, although such legislation had been in vogue in many other countries since the sixteenth century. A great outcry was raised here at the time and continued for years afterwards. Many thought that this legislation was directed expressly against Protestants, though nothing is further from the truth. The fact is that, even if there were not one Protestant in existence, this law would remain in force. Let me explain it:

The grand old Church ·has had nineteen hundred years of experience, and she knows what laws are most conducive to the general good of her subjects. She never even tries to impose laws on those who are not her subjects, that is, on non-baptized persons. But she has a divine right to legislate for all who have been baptized, even though they may not recognize her authority. Still, the "Ne Temere" Decree was promulgated especially for Catholics, and it only indirectly affects non-Catholics.

As far back as the sixteenth century (the Church already had had a very long experience of human nature), the Council of Trent (a universal Council of Bishops) enacted, amongst other salutary laws, the Decree "Tametsi" and left it to the Bishops of the various countries to promulgate it. The "Ne Temere" Decree was simply the promulgation of this old law in these new countries. And this legislation was made particularly for Catholics.

The Church realized the danger of certain persons, bent on marrying even when there were impediments in the way, going off to a strange parish and requesting the pastor of such a parish to perform the marriage. Now, because a parish priest knows his own parishioners better than any other pastor, and because a bishop knows his own flock better than any other bishop, and also because a parish priest can more easily investigate the condition of his own parishioners, and a bishop can more effectively ascertain the condition of his own subjects, the Church, in order to obviate or prevent irregular or invalid marriages, decreed that marriage of her subjects should be performed by the pastor or the bishop of the persons to be married, or elsewhere only with the permission of such pastor or bishop. Surely this is eminently reasonable. That was the substance of the Decree "Tametsi."

The "Ne Temere" Decree, now embodied in the New Code of Ecclesiastical Law, simply means that no Catholic can be validly married except by a parish priest or a bishop or by a priest delegated by one of them—the pastor of the parish or the bishop of the diocese where the marriage takes place. If the parties belong to another parish, the priest who performs the marriage is commanded to get permission from the pastor of that parish. There must also be two witnesses to the marriage. There are some differences between the Decree "Tametsi" and the Decree "Ne Temere," but I need not burden you with them, for I am not giving you a treatise on Canon Law.

It suffices for you to see that the Church has authority to make diriment impediments to marriage and also to prescribe **how** the marriage of her own subjects must be performed (that is, to prescribe the **form**) in order to be a valid sacramental contract. And she prescribes, under pain of nullity, that, where at least one of the contracting parties is a Catholic, the marriage must be performed before the Bishop (or Vicar General) of the diocese, or the pastor of the parish, where the marriage takes place, and in the presence of two witnesses. For the **lawfulness** of marriage, the Church prescribes that, when the parties belong to another parish than that in which they wish to be married, the officiating priest must have the permission of the pastor of the contracting parties.

To show you, conclusively, my dear convert, that such legislation is not directed against Protestants, let me tell you that if I, a Catholic priest living in Kensington, N.S.W., celebrated here **a marriage of two Catholics** without first obtaining delegation or permission from the parish priest of Kensington (or from the Archbishop of Sydney), such marriage would be null and void. How, then, can it be reasonably objected that the legislation I have spoken of was directed against Protestants? I am sure that, if our non-Catholic friends fully grasped the matter, they would readily admit that the Church, in making such a law, acted most reasonably.

CHAPTER XXVII.

IMPEDIMENTS TO MATRIMONY

IN our last chat, my dear convert, I explained the Church's authority over the marriage of baptized persons and showed that she had the right to enact laws which would render marriage in certain circumstances either invalid or unlawful—that she could establish impediments to matrimony. But you must not understand from what I said in that chat that impediments to marriage result only from Church legislation, for some obstacles to valid or lawful marriage proceed from the very law of nature or from the positive law of God. In order to bring home to you more easily and clearly still the meaning of matrimonial impediments, I shall give you a simple illustration.

IMPEDIMENTS ILLUSTRATED OR EXEMPLIFIED

Let us suppose two boys out for a walk on a mountain. Suddenly they come to a cave which they would like to enter. But they notice a very large boulder blocking the mouth of the cave—a rock so large that no human being could have placed it there. This boulder, which was put there by nature, is a **natural impediment** to the boys' entrance into the cave. In a similar way there are natural impediments to marriage. The Church has not put them there; they were established by the very law of nature, which comes from God. For example, a brother and a sister cannot validly marry each other, for that is against the very law of nature, which allowed such a marriage only at the very beginning of the human race when it was necessary for the propagation of mankind. (Thus Cain must have married a sister—the Bible tells us that Adam had daughters as well as sons.) One who has not yet reached the age of reason, e.g., a child of five could not validly marry, for that is against the very law of nature which requires a certain knowledge and consent for the matrimonial contract which an infant has not yet attained.

Let us suppose that later on the two boys of whom I am speaking are going down the mountain and come to a cabin or little house which also they wish to enter. They try to open the door, but it is locked from the inside. That locked door is an impediment to their entrance into the house. But, since it was put there by a human being, it is a **human impediment.** This is an example of an ecclesiastical impediment to marriage—an obstacle put there by the Church's legislation, e.g., blood relationship not forbidden by the natural or divine law (cousin relationship).

Lastly, we shall suppose that, as the boys come home, they find that their father has tied a rope to some pegs which he has driven in the ground around a bed of strawberries, and that he has put up a notice forbidding his children take any strawberries. But the boys climb over or crawl under the rope and steal some strawberries. You see that in this case there was an impediment which did not completely block the boys from getting to the strawberry bed. Yet the boys did wrong, for they disobeyed their father. This rope fence is an illustration of an impediment which does not annul (render null and void) a marriage, but simply makes it unlawful or sinful. The best known example of such a marriage impediment is that of **mixed religion,** which means that the Church forbids marriage between a Catholic and a baptized non-

Catholic. Persons who would contract such a marriage in spite of the Church (if we could suppose them to follow the prescribed form by deceiving a pastor) would be truly married though the marriage would be unlawful. If a Catholic wishes to marry a non-Catholic who is **not baptized**, there exists the impediment known as difference of worship, which is an annulling impediment. Both kinds of impediments, those which are called diriment or annulling impediments and those which are known as prohibitory impediments, may proceed from the law of God or from the law of the Church: in the former case they are said to be of **divine law**, and in the latter of **ecclesiastical law.**

WHY THE CHURCH FORBIDS MIXED MARRIAGES

We shall consider together two impediments, mixed religion and difference of worship, the former prohibitory, the latter annulling (as I have already explained). I am considering these two together because the reasons for which the Church has decreed them are practically the same, although the case is more serious where the non-Catholic is not even a Christian, but is a Jew, a Mahometan (or Mohammedan), or an infidel (or pagan). The great reason why the Church opposes marriage between a Catholic and a non-Catholic is that, in such marriages, there is often serious danger to the faith of the Catholic party and of the children born of such marriages. The Church, like a loving, solicitous mother, must watch over the faith of all her members and see that they keep this precious gift and pass it on to their children. Sad experience shows how many souls have been wrecked, have lost the faith, or given it up (at least the practice of it) through mixed marriages, and how many lovely children have been born and brought up without the true faith because of such marriages.

MEANING OF A DISPENSATION

For a serious reason the Church may grant a dispensation to a Catholic to marry a non-Catholic. A dispensation means relaxing or suspending a law in a certain case. Sometimes it is only to prevent a greater evil that the Church grants such a dispensation. And always, before granting it, she requires the non-Catholic party to promise (generally in writing) not to interfere with the Catholic party's right or freedom to practice the faith, and also to promise to allow all the children born of the marriage to be brought up and educated as Catholics. She also commands the Catholic party to strive to convert the non-Catholic party to the true faith.

If anyone objected to the Church's marriage legislation, I should answer: Why, even a football club or a tennis club or a social club claims the right to make rules for its members and to enforce them under pain of expulsion or other penalty; and will you deny the same right to the greatest society the world has ever seen—the Catholic Church?

Someone may say: "But I have known happy mixed marriages, where the children are fervent Catholics and the non-Catholic is most honorable." Yes, I, too, have known such marriages, and I appreciate the honor and chivalry and goodness of the non-Catholic party. But such marriages are the exception, not the rule.

TWO TERRIBLE EVILS: DIVORCE AND BIRTH PREVENTION

I have dealt with divorce in our previous chat; at least I have shown that it is opposed to the Divine Law. But I wish to add that it is also one of the greatest evils which afflict modern society. Even if God had not revealed to us its sinfulness, right reason would show us its hideousness. The very thought of deliberately breaking up a home and leaving innocent little children fatherless or motherless, or—worse still—foisting on them a man or woman who cannot be regarded even as a step-father, is revolting to the human heart.

Birth prevention, so widely advocated nowadays by persons with little or no religion, is also condemned by the Law of God, which His infallible Church has clearly made known to us. We find that, in the Old Law, God struck Onan dead for this. abominable sin. It is against the very law of nature, and it lowers man below the brute creation, for irrational animals instinctively obey the laws of Nature imposed by their Creator.

Perhaps you will tell me that you know Catholics who practice birth prevention. Well, my dear friend, we do not claim that all Catholics are saints, or even that all Catholics observe the Law of God or of the Church. Remember that, when He spoke of "the Kingdom of Heaven" (the Church), Christ compared it to a net containing both good and bad fishes. If a Catholic is practicing birth prevention, he or she cannot lawfully receive the Sacraments; to go to Confession and receive Holy Communion without a change of heart would be to make a sacrilegious confession and receive Holy Communion unworthily. I should have far more respect for such a Catholic (one who is practicing birth prevention), if he or she abstained from the Sacraments, for it is a lesser evil not to receive the Sacraments than to receive them sacrilegiously. No priest can validly absolve one guilty of birth prevention unless such a person is really determined to give up this vile practice.

You know now, my dear convert, that, when you become a Catholic, divorce is absolutely out of the question and that, under pain of being denied absolution and excluded from Holy Communion, you must be determined never to frustrate the laws of Nature in your conjugal relations. A Protestant once had a friendly chat with me, telling me that he wished to become a Catholic, but asking if he could still marry a divorced woman whom he loved. He would not promise to give her up, and so I had to refuse to receive him into the Church. We priests cannot whittle down the law of God. Likewise, I have known of non-Catholics who were willing to become Catholics, but who declared that they would continue to practice birth prevention, for they considered it too hard to give up the practice. Of course, they could not be received into the Church while they persisted in that state of mind and will.

But I am sure, my dear friend, that you, who are convinced that the Catholic Church is the one true Church and have decided to embrace the Catholic Religion, will, when you enter the fold, courageously carry out all God's commands and obey the laws of the Church relying on God's abundant graces and pondering on Christ's words: "What doth it profit a man if he gain the whole world and suffer the loss of his own soul?"

CHAPTER XXVIII.

DEVOTION TO THE BLESSED VIRGIN

BEFORE explaining to you, my dear friend, Catholic doctrine and practice regarding the Blessed Virgin Mary, let me state two truths which the Church teaches most emphatically: (1) God alone, the Supreme, Infinite Being, must be adored. To adore any creature, however exalted, would be to commit **idolatry.** It is simply absurd and also grossly unfair to say that Catholics adore Mary. (2) Jesus Christ alone is our Mediator of Redemption. He alone, by His supreme sacrifice, of infinite value, redeemed and ransomed mankind.

WHAT HONOR MAY BE SHOWN TO MARY?

If God alone is to be adored; if Christ alone is to be worshipped as our Mediator of Redemption, may any honor be shown to Mary, the Mother of Jesus; and, if so, what kind of honor?

There is an innate law engraven on the human heart which dictates that special honor should be shown to creatures who are clothed with a special dignity. Children must honor their parents; servants must revere their masters; soldiers must respect their officers; subjects must show loyalty to their rulers. God Himself has, in fact, positively commanded, in His revelation to man, this honor which the natural law prescribes. Our non-Catholic friends, following reason and accepting the teaching of the Bible, cannot but admit this principle or truth. Thus it is as clear as day that, besides the supreme honor which we give God, and which we term adoration, there is an inferior honor which we not only may but must show to all creatures who are clothed with special dignity.

What, then, must be said of our duty of honoring the Blessed Virgin Mary, whose dignity as far transcends that of any other creature as heaven excels earth; whose holiness as far surpasses that of the highest seraph as the splendor of the sun surpasses the brightness of the moon; whom God Himself has favored and honored incomparably more than any other creature that has come forth from His almighty hands? Mary was chosen out of all possible creatures for the highest office that Omnipotence can confer on a finite being—the Divine Motherhood. From her virginal flesh the Eternal Son of God drew His body; She conceived God the Son in His human nature and brought Him forth and nurtured Him. Since there is but one Person in the God-man, Mary is truly called the Mother of God, for She conceived and brought forth God in His human nature. It is obvious that, when we call Her the Mother of God, we do not for a moment imply that Mary produced the Divine Nature, which is eternal. But She conceived and brought forth Him who is truly God, and therefore Mary must be called the Mother of God, as the great Council of Ephesus solemnly defined in the year 431, eleven centuries before Protestantism sprang up to reject devotion to Mary.

Of all creatures Mary has the unique privilege of **adoring Her own Child.** To Mary alone can God the Son address the sweet title, **Mother!** What a marvelous dignity, then, was conferred on the humble **Virgin of Nazareth!**

THE SCRIPTURES TEACH DEVOTION TO MARY

I ask you, my dear friend, to read carefully the first chapter of the Gospel of St. Luke, verse 26 to verse 55. It is very hard to understand how any Christian can study this passage and then refuse to honor Mary. Why, the "Hail Mary," which Catholics love to address to the Blessed Virgin, is explicitly given there; part of it was said by the Angel Gabriel and part by Elizabeth. The Angel was inspired by God and Elizabeth "was filled with the Holy Ghost" (v. 41). Let us put together the words which the Angel Gabriel and Elizabeth addressed to Mary: "Hail, full of grace, the Lord is with thee: blessed are thou among women" (v. 28). "Blessed are thou among women, and blessed is the fruit of thy womb." Here we have the salutation which Catholics address to Mary. The only addition we have made are the two names, "Mary" and "Jesus." So that, in saying the "Hail, Mary," Catholics are explicitly following the Bible. I shall deal with the second part of this prayer presently.

You will notice, my dear friend, that Mary in that sublime canticle known as the **Magnificat,** which is recorded by the inspired writer from verse 46 to 55, declared: "Behold from henceforth all generations shall call me blessed" (v. 48). Who, I ask, fulfil this prophecy—those who refuse to apply the adjective **blessed** to the Virgin Mary, or Catholics, who love to call Mary the Blessed Virgin?

INVOCATION OF MARY

Not only do we honor Mary; we also invoke Her or ask Her intercession. Some objectors say that we should pray to God alone. Well, Catholics certainly pray directly to God, for they regard the "Our Father" as the best and most beautiful of all prayers and frequently recite it. But they pray also to Mary, asking Her to intercede for them with Her Divine Son.

Our non-Catholic friends ask one another's prayers, and in this we praise them. But, if I may say to a sinner on this earth, and he may say to me, another sinner, "Pray for me," for what reason may we not say to the sinless Mother of God enthroned in heaven, "Pray for us"? If St. Paul asked the Romans to "help him in their prayers for him to God" (Romans XV., 16); if he wrote to the Thessalonians, "Pray for us," why may we not ask Mary, who is far holier and nearer to God than the Roman and Thessalonian converts, to "pray for us"? In fact, we read in the Old Testament that God positively commanded Eliphaz and his two friends to go to the holy man Job and seek his intercession: "My servant Job shall pray for you; his face I will accept, that folly be not imputed to you" (Job XLII., 8).

Therefore Catholics act aright when they say: "Holy Mary, Mother of God, pray for us sinners now and at the hour of our death."

STATUES AND PICTURES OF MARY

But why, someone may ask, do Catholics have statues or pictures of Mary in their churches and homes? Is it not against the first (or second) commandment to make graven images? No, it is against God's laws to adore images, not to make them; otherwise we should have to abolish all such things as dolls, for are they not "graven images"? And does anyone imagine that it is against the first commandment to make dolls or to give them to children? God even commanded the making of certain images in the Old Law, as we read in various parts of the Old Testament. For instance, he ordered Moses to make two cherubim (angels) of beaten gold (Exodus XXV., 18).

If non-Catholics approve of the making and erecting of statues of Queen Victoria or King Edward or General MacArthur or Charles Dickens or Roosevelt (and in this we agree with them), how can they possibly see anything objectionable in making a statue of the Blessed Virgin, Mother of the King of kings, and putting it in a prominent place? We ask our friends outside the Church to be fair and not to attempt playing: "Heads I win, and tails you lose."

As to the custom of lighting candles and placing vases of flowers before the statue or picture of the Blessed Virgin, no person can reasonably object to this practice who would approve of a college boarder plucking flowers, arranging them nicely in vases, and putting them in front of her mother's photo, which she had placed on the mantelpiece in her room. If the latter is a praiseworthy practice—as every person endowed with reason and affection admits—surely the former custom is equally laudable. Likewise, if a child may laudably kiss the photo of her absent mother, in order to show her love for her (though the child well knows that the photo itself is an inanimate, unresponsive object), so Catholics are worthy of praise when they kiss a picture or statue of Mary in order to express the love they have for the living Queen of Heaven, whom the image represents.

HONORING SAINTS AND VENERATING THEIR RELICS

What I have said, my dear friend, of devotion to the Blessed Virgin applies in a lesser degree to honoring and invoking saints. On its calendar of saints the Church inscribes the names of martyrs—those who have died for the faith—and extraordinarily holy persons, into whose lives she has made a very minute, most careful inquiry. Now, as a nation honors its heroes and erects their statues in conspicuous places, so the Church has ever honored those Christian heroes who have attained a sublime degree of holiness. And, as all classes of persons, even those who have no religion, venerate the remains of their dear departed ones and treasure souvenirs of them—something that was intimately associated with them in life—so do we venerate the remains of martyrs and saints and treasure their relics—things that were closely associated with them.

It is strange how inconsistent persons can be who object to Catholic practices. Communists, who sneer at Catholic veneration of the relics of saints, pay extraordinary honor to the mummified corpse of Lenin. People who would criticize Catholics for treasuring relics of a martyr vied with one another to grab a cigarette butt that fell from the lips of Robert Taylor, the movie star, as he stood on the balcony of a London hotel!

PROTESTANT POETS AND DEVOTION TO MARY

Devotion to Mary is so beautiful a practice and fits in so harmoniously in the plan of the Christian religion, that the Christian soul, untrammelled or untainted by prejudice, instinctively recognizes its truth. I have not infrequently been struck by the fact that Protestant children, who have as yet been given no bias against this devotion, quickly perceive its loveliness and are strongly attracted by it when once they are given even an elementary idea of it. And even more mature non-Catholic children are sometimes at a loss to know why they have been turned against such a sweet, appealing devotion. I once heard a Presbyterian girl of twelve, who had seen a picture of Our Lady of Good Counsel, ask her mother: "Why don't Protestants honor the Mother of Jesus?"

Poetry helps men to shed prejudice, and so we find

certain Protestant poets, in their moments of poetic rapture, writing exquisite things about the Blessed Virgin. The following beautiful lines come from the pen of Wordsworth:—

"Mother whose virgin bosom was uncrossed
With the least shade of thought to sin allied.
Woman! above all women glorified,
Our tainted nature's solitary boast;
Purer than foam on central ocean tossed;
Brighter than eastern skies at daybreak strewn
With fancied roses; than unblemished moon
Before her wane begins on heaven's blue coast."

Longfellow, another non-Catholic poet, has given us a lovely poem:

"This is indeed the Blessed Mary's land!
Virgin and Mother of our dear Redeemer;
All hearts are touched and softened at her name;
Alike the bandit, with the bloody hand,
The priest, the prince, the scholar, and the peasant,
The man of deeds, the visionary dreamer,
Pay homage to her as one ever present!
And even as children who have much offended
A too-indulgent father, in great shame,
Penitent, and yet not daring unattended
To go into his presence, at the gate
Speak with their sister, and confiding wait
Till she goes in before and intercedes;
So men, repenting of their evil deeds,
And yet, not venturing rashly to draw near
With their requests an angry father's ear,
Offer to her their prayers and their confession,
And she for them in heaven makes intercession.
And if our faith had given us nothing more
Than this example of all womanhood,
So mild, so merciful, so strong, so good,
So patient, peaceful, loyal, loving, pure,
This were enough to prove it higher and truer
Than all the creeds the world had known before."

CHAPTER XXIX.

PURGATORY

THE moment after death occurs—the moment, that is, at which the human soul departs from the human body—judgment is pronounced by God. "It is appointed unto men once to die, and after this the judgment" (Hebrews IX., 27). That sentence is irrevocable; the soul is now in a state of eternal salvation or everlasting damnation. There is no such thing as a reprieve after death—another chance in the next life. We are granted abundant opportunities in the present life, during which God is ever calling us to Himself and showing the greatest sinners unbounded patience and, if they repent, unbounded mercy. But, as soon as death occurs, the irreversible sentence is pronounced by the just judge of mankind.

THE MEANING OF HELL

Until comparatively recent times practically all Protestants believed that hell, as well as heaven, exists in the future life. But nowadays many non-Catholics have ceased to accept the doctrine of eternal punishment. However, whether or not we choose to believe it will not alter the reality. One may refuse to believe that a terrific war is being waged in Europe at the present time, but such complacent mentality will not change the awful reality. I admit that the doctrine of everlasting punishment is a fearful truth, but, since God has clearly revealed it, we must assent to it, however unpalatable it may be. God is infinite, and so He does things on a scale which bewilders our poor finite minds. The reward He confers on those who serve Him is eternal and indescribable; the punishment He metes out in eternity to those who have deliberately rejected Him in this life is everlasting and unspeakable.

Hell consists essentially in the **eternal loss of God.** The sinner refused to have God in this life—God refuses to have that soul in eternity. In this life a sinner may distract himself with many occupations and recreations; he may indulge in various pleasures, enjoy earthly honors, acquire riches, busy himself with varied pursuits. But in eternity there will be none of these earthly distractions or diversions, and, if the soul misses God, it will experience an eternal void such as we cannot imagine. Black, hopeless, unceasing despair will engulf it, and everlasting remorse will consume it without destroying it, for the human soul is immortal.

The Catholic Church teaches as an article of faith that the pain of loss, which I have just explained, is essential to hell. The lost soul will never see or enjoy God, for whom it was created, and in whom alone it could have found perfect happiness, everlasting beatitude. In place of that everlasting happiness, to which it was destined, it will experience eternal misery and endless suffering.

The Sacred Scriptures speak of hell not only as the eternal loss of God, but also as an unending abode of fire which tortures the soul. Though the Church has not defined that this fire is real, still constant tradition thus interprets it, and it is the common teaching of theologians. But the thought alone of the everlasting loss of the vision or possession of God, the one Object that could possibly make us happy, is something truly appalling, and should constantly deter us from committing sin, at least mortal or grave sin, which severs our friendship with God. Hell may, in fact, be described as the state of mortal sin rendered eternal.

You may read the Gospels for yourself, my dear convert, and see how often Christ clearly spoke of the eternity of hell.

WHAT IS HEAVEN?

Heaven is the state or abode of eternal blessedness. It consists essentially in the everlasting face to face vision of God, the eternal rapturous or ecstatic love of God, and the endless enjoyment of God. In a word, it consists in the **beatific vision**—the clear, immediate, face to face vision of God as God sees Himself. As a result of that vision the soul is borne to God by the irresistible impulse of ecstatic love (known as beatific love), and in that vision and love it eternally enjoys God as He enjoys Himself.

Heaven means the absence of all pain and sorrow and the presence of all good. The soul is literally deluged with delight. It is free from all care and anxiety, all suffering and sorrow; it enjoys perennial peace, "the peace which surpasseth all understanding"; it is no longer subject to labor or toil, but enjoys sweet, "eternal rest"; it is united inseparably with the glorified souls of loved ones who have gone before it into the vision of the Godhead; on the redeemed soul is shed the inexpressible ardor of myriads of saints and angels; it basks beneath the everlasting smile of Mary, the Mother of God and our Mother; it is unceasingly thrilled beyond expression by the loving presence and companionship of our glorified Divine Redeemer; it sees God as God sees Himself, loves God as God loves Himself, enjoys God as God enjoys Himself, and in that vision and love and enjoyment perennially experiences a happiness, an ecstasy, a beatific union with God, of which we can, in this life, where "we see through a glass dimly," form but a very feeble conception. "Eye hath not seen, nor ear heard, neither hath it entered into the heart of man to conceive what things God hath prepared for those who love Him."

PURGATORY

Although each soul is irrevocably judged the moment it leaves the body and is thus put at once and for ever in a state of damnation or salvation, it does not follow that a soul that is saved must be admitted at once into the beatific vision. When we consider the dazzling holiness of God, before whom the choirs of Angels ever sing, "Holy, Holy, Holy," and into whose unveiled presence "there shall not enter anything defiled," and when we remember that even a just man may be stained with blemishes, we are not surprised that God requires of many a soul in the state of grace that it should be purified, or should expiate fully its every fault, before being admitted into His beatific presence.

TEMPORAL PUNISHMENT DUE TO VENIAL SIN

St. John writes: "If we say we have no sin, we deceive ourselves, and the truth is not in us" (1 John I., 8). And St. James writes: "In many things we all offend" (James III., 2). It is evident that the sin spoken of by these two Apostles is not necessarily grave sin, for it is not true that all the faithful, even the Apostles, are guilty of mortal sin. There must, therefore, be lesser sins—those faults into which even a just man may fall. Yet such faults defile or stain the soul, which is accordingly not pure enough, while tarnished with such stains, to be admitted to the eternal embrace of God. Now, if such a soul has not fully expiated such sins (or even had them forgiven) before it passed out of the body, what will be its fate? God cannot in justice condemn it to hell, for the soul is in the state of grace—is in God's friendship. Yet such a soul is not pure or holy enough to be admitted at once to heaven—to the face to face vision of God. Hence there **must** be a third state after death, where such souls are purified from these lesser sins.

Our Lord alluded to the remission of such sins "in the world to come" (Matt. XII., 32). The fact that He spoke of a certain sin not being forgiven "either in this world or in the world to come" implies, as St. Augustine and St. Gregory show, that there are some sins (venial sins) which may be remitted in the world to come, and that there must, therefore, be an intermediate state of purification or expiation, which we call purgatory.

TEMPORAL PUNISHMENT DUE TO FORGIVEN MORTAL SIN

When God forgives sin, He does not always acquit the sinner of all debt to His offended Majesty. In the case of mortal sin, He forgives the **guilt** of the sin and the **eternal punishment** due to it; but He often requires **a temporal debt** (a debt of temporal punishment—temporal expiation) to be paid. We see this in the case of David. Although God forgave David his heinous sin (his double mortal sin), yet He exacted of this king a severe temporal punishment—the death of his child.

Now, it may be that a sinner has not completely expiated his forgiven mortal (or even venial) sins in this life, and that his soul appears before the Eternal Judge, justified indeed, but laden with the full debt of temporal punishment which it had not paid in this life. Such a soul cannot be condemned to hell, for it is in God's friendship, nor can it be admitted at once to the everlasting vision of God; hence it must be detained for a time in a third or intermediate state where it may expiate its forgiven sins. Of this state or abode Christ spoke when He called it a prison in which the soul is detained until it pays the last farthing—until it completely satisfies God's justice. "Amen I say to thee, thou shalt not go out from thence till thou repay the last farthing." The prison He here speaks of cannot be hell, for hell is eternal—there is no such thing as merely remaining there until the soul pays the last farthing.

St. Paul also alludes to Purgatory when he states that some "shall be saved, yet so as by fire" (1 Cor. III., 15). Eleven centuries before Protestantism arose to deny Purgatory, which had been taught as a Christian truth from apostolic times, St. Augustine, commenting on this text of St. Paul, explains this fire as distinct from that of hell and as purifying or cleansing those souls which are saved by fire.

PRAYER FOR THE DEAD IS BASED ON THE DOCTRINE OF PURGATORY

If there were no purgatory, prayers for the dead would be worse than useless. We cannot help the blessed, for they are already enjoying the vision of God. Nor can our prayers assist the reprobate or damned, for their lot is irremediable: "Too late, too late! Ye cannot enter now." For what souls, then, do we pray? For those who are undergoing their period of expiation prior to their admission into the vision of God—that is, for the souls in Purgatory.

The practice of praying for the dead is, in fact, older than Christianity. We find that God's chosen people in the Old Testament prayed for the dead. This is recorded clearly in the second Book of Machabees, whose genuine historical authority, even though they unreasonably reject its inspired character, non-Catholics cannot deny. I draw your attention, my dear friend, to the following striking passage:

"And making a gathering, he (Judas Machabeus) sent twelve thousand drachms of silver to Jerusalem for sacrifice to be offered for the sins of the dead, thinking well and religiously concerning the resurrection.

"(For if he had not hoped that they that were slain should rise again, it would have seemed superfluous and vain to pray for the dead.)

"And because he considered that they who had fallen asleep with godliness had great grace laid up for them.

"It is therefore a holy and wholesome thought to pray for the dead, that they may be loosed from their sins" (2 Mach. XII., 43-46).

In the Christian Church prayer and sacrifice have been offered up for the dead from the earliest times. You will recall the beautiful passage I quoted for you from the writings of St. Cyril of Jerusalem, who wrote as early as the middle half of the fourth century. The passage referred to the Sacrifice of the Mass, but I now draw your attention particularly to this sentence: "For all amongst us who have already departed this life we pray, since we believe that it will be of the greatest benefit to them if, in the presence of this holy and tremendous sacrifice, we make our petitions for them."

I could give you, my dear convert, many quotations from the early Fathers and the ancient Liturgies to show that the Church has ever prayed for the dead. But I shall conclude with a striking passage from the great Doctor, St. Augustine of Hippo, who died in the year 430:

"Some (of the faithful) are relieved by the piety of their living friends, when the sacrifice of the Mediator is offered for them, or alms are distributed; but these suffrages benefit those who, while they were living, merited that these helps should later be of avail to them: for there is a certain way of living which is not so good as not to require these helps after death, nor so bad as not to be assisted by them after death."

The following words of Augustine are equally clear and explicitly mention **purgatory:**

"The more or less they have been attached to earthly things, the more slowly or more speedily are they saved by a certain purgatorial fire."

In concluding this chat, my dear friend, I wish to stress the truth that the Catholic doctrine of purgatory shows that the Catholic Church has a more exalted conception of God's holiness and justice and the malice of sin than has any non-Catholic denomination which rejects this doctrine.

CHAPTER XXX.

FINAL CHAT: PREPARATION FOR RECEPTION

YOU have, my dear convert, patiently followed the course of instruction which I have gladly given you. I appreciate your earnestness and your fervor, and I congratulate you on your fidelity in coming to listen to these Chats. You are now ready to be received into the Church, and I shall explain to you what the ceremony of reception is. When a convert has never been baptized at all, the ceremony of admission into the Catholic Church consists in receiving the Sacrament of Baptism. When a convert has been validly baptized in another Christian denomination, he makes the requisite Profession of Faith, is absolved from excommunication, and then goes to confession. If the convert has been already baptized in another denomination, but there is serious doubt as to whether the baptism was properly administered, or if there is doubt as to whether the convert was ever baptized, then the ceremony of reception requires four things: (1) Profession of Faith, (2) Absolution from Excommunication, (3) Conditional Baptism—Baptism, that is, administered conditionally, (4) Confession and Conditional Absolution (absolution given conditionally). All this I must now explain.

BAPTISM

I have already spoken of Baptism when explaining to you the meaning of a Sacrament. Baptism is the most important of all the sacraments, though not the greatest, for it is obvious that the Blessed Eucharist is the greatest or the highest in dignity. But Baptism is the most important because it is absolutely necessary for salvation, so that, unless one receives this sacrament actually or in desire, or its equivalent, the grace of martyrdom (which is called Baptism of blood), one cannot possibly be saved. Baptism of desire means the wish to receive Baptism, but not the mere wish or desire of Baptism, as some people imagine, for this desire must be contained explicitly or implicitly in an **Act of Perfect Contrition or Perfect Charity.** Perfect charity means love of God above all things for His own sake—love of Him because He is infinitely good in Himself, infinitely beautiful, holy, sweet, lovable. And sorrow for displeasing God because He is so good in Himself—so beautiful, so lovable, so holy, so sweet, so perfect—and sin insults or offends or grieves Him, is called perfect contrition. But, my dear friend, since you have already read the whole Catechism carefully several times, you need no further explanation of contrition.

There is another reason why Baptism is the most important sacrament: unless a person is validly or truly baptized (in this case baptism of desire will not suffice), he cannot validly receive the other sacraments.

Sacramental Baptism may be validly administered in three ways—by **immersion** (plunging a person in water), **affusion** (pouring water on the head—on the forehead—of a person), and **aspersion** (sprinkling the head—the face—with water so that it **flows**). While the person is immersed or has the water poured on him or is sprinkled, the minister (the person, that is, who administers the sacrament) must say distinctly: "I baptize thee in the name of the Father and of the Son and of the Holy Ghost."

Now, my dear friend, anyone may baptize validly. But he must rightly apply the water, say the right words and say them at the same time as he applies the water, and have the right intention—the intention of doing what Christ prescribed or intended when He instituted the sacrament (or what the Church intends). But, although many Protestant ministers baptize, we are often doubtful as to whether they do so validly (or truly or properly, as I have explained). And not a few of them do not consider Baptism necessary. I talked with a Methodist mother recently and she told me that not one of her children was baptized, that she did not see any need for it, and that her minister agreed with her. I knew personally a Methodist local preacher locally who told me he had never been baptized and that he was not anxious about the matter, for he saw no need for Baptism. Because we are often doubtful whether a convert has ever been baptized, or doubtful whether he has been properly (or validly) baptized, we often administer **conditional Baptism** when receiving him (or her) into the Church. In fact, since such loose notions now prevail outside the Catholic Church concerning the necessity of Baptism, and because even those who administer it are sometimes remiss or careless or ignorant regarding the true rite of Baptism, we always give a convert conditional Baptism unless we are certain of two things: (1) that he was baptized, and (2) that the minister rightly applied the water, said the right words at the same time, and had the right intention. In your case, my dear friend, all our inquiries leave your Baptism in doubt, and so I shall administer to you this important sacrament conditionally.

We administer conditional Baptism by pouring water on the forehead of the convert and saying at the same time: "If thou are not baptized, I baptize thee in the name of the Father and of the Son and of the Holy Ghost." It would not do to let you go through life with only a doubtful Baptism; therefore I shall make sure by giving you conditional Baptism. If you have already validly received this sacrament; what I now do for you will not be a sacrament at all; if you have never been properly baptized, you will now truly receive the Sacrament of Baptism.

PROFESSION OF FAITH

No adult can be received into the Catholic Church unless he has faith. I mean that it would be unlawful to admit him. If you were not absolutely convinced that the Catholic Church is the one true Church; if you did not whole-heartedly believe all that the Catholic Church believes and teaches, I should not admit you into the Church. But, since I know from our chats that you firmly believe all that the Church teaches and I recognize that you quite freely seek admission, I shall gladly receive you. But the Church insists that one who has been validly or even doubtfully baptized in another denomination must make a Profession of Faith before being admitted. This Profession must be made under oath; you will touch the Holy Gospels while making it, thus calling God to witness what you are declaring or professing.

I shall now read to you the Profession of Faith, which you will presently make personally:

Touching the holy Gospels of God with my hand, and enlightened by divine grace, I ———— confess the faith which the Catholic, Apostolic, Roman Church proposes. I believe that this Church is the one true Church which Jesus Christ established on earth, and I submit myself to it with my whole heart.

I believe in God the Father Almighty, Creator of heaven and earth; and in Jesus Christ, His only Son,

Our Lord; who was conceived by the Holy Ghost, born of the Virgin Mary, suffered under Pontius Pilate, was crucified, died and was buried; He descended into hell; the third day He rose again from the dead. He ascended into heaven, sitteth at the right hand of God the Father Almighty; from thence He shall come to judge the living and the dead. I believe in the Holy Ghost; the holy Catholic Church; the communion of saints; the forgiveness of sins; the resurrection of the body and life everlasting. Amen.

I believe that seven sacraments were instituted by Jesus Christ for the salvation of the human race, namely, Baptism, Confirmation, Eucharist, Penance, Extreme Unction, Order, and Matrimony.

I believe that the Roman Pontiff is the vicar of Jesus Christ on earth, the visible Supreme Head of the whole Church, who teaches infallibly what is to be believed and done.

I believe moreover all that the Holy, Catholic, Apostolic, and Roman Church defines and declares to be believed. I adhere to this Church with my whole heart, and I reject all the errors and schisms condemned by it.

So help me God and these His holy Gospels which I touch with my hand.

ABSOLUTION FROM EXCOMMUNICATION

I need not say much to you, my dear friend, about absolution from excommunication, for I know from the dispositions you have shown and have, from what you candidly tell me, had during your past life, that, although you have the frailties of human nature, you have not wilfully rebelled or revolted against or rejected, what you apprehended as God's teaching and God's law. As soon as you recognized the Catholic

Church as Christ's own Church, you assured me that you would become a Catholic as soon as I saw fit to receive you. Excommunication is incurred only by baptized persons who knowingly and advertently and wilfully reject the teaching of the Catholic Church which they recognize as the true Church. Excommunication is a penalty which the Church imposes on rebellious subjects for certain sins, and which excludes them from the communion of the faithful. Even a tennis club or a social club has its own kind of excommunication.

Now, my dear convert, you must realize the possibility and even the probability of some non-Catholics having incurred the censure or penalty of excommunication. In certain very rare cases there could be, in fact, a certainty. But the vast majority of those whom we receive into the Church have never incurred it. However, in order to remove every possible obstacle to union with the Mother Church, what may be termed conditional absolution from excommunication is given after the convert recites the Profession of Faith.

The formula of absolution, pronounced in Latin, is thus translated: "By the apostolic authority, which I exercise in this matter, I absolve you from the bond of excommunication which you may have incurred, and I restore you to the holy sacraments of the Church, to the communion and unity of the faithful, in the name of the Father and of the Son and of the Holy Ghost. Amen."

CONFESSION AND CONDITIONAL ABSOLUTION

I explained to you all about confession when we were chatting over the Sacrament of Penance. But I must now add a few words about your first confession. If you had never been baptized, there would be no question of confession when you were being received into the Church. I have sometimes—only on a few occasions—received into the Church adults—one was an old man, and he died suddenly on the day of his first Holy Communion—who had never been baptized in any denomination. In these cases the reception into the Church was a very simple matter. No Profession of Faith was required; no Absolution from Excommunication; no confession or conditional absolution, but simply the administration of Baptism (with all the accompanying ceremonies). In such cases Baptism blots out not only original sin (of which I told you long since) and all actual or personal sins, but also all the temporal punishment due to forgiven actual sin, so that, if a convert died immediately after this absolute (unconditional) Baptism, his (or her) soul would be admitted **at once** into the eternal beatific vision of the Godhead—that is, would go immediately to heaven without passing through purgatory.

But, my dear friend, inquiries show that **you** have **probably** been baptized validly already. So I can give you only **conditional** Baptism. But we must make **sure** of your getting the state of grace or the supernatural friendship of God. Therefore you must receive also **conditional** absolution of all the actual sins on your soul, and to receive this, you will need to go to confession. But your confession will be just like having a quiet, confidential chat with a trusty, sympathetic friend, and you may choose any priest for your confession. After you receive conditional absolution, you will be able to say: "Either my conditional baptism or my conditional absolution was valid; therefore I am now certain (morally certain) that I am in the state of grace."

You will then prepare lovingly and **trustfully for**

your first Holy Communion, which you should receive a day or two after your reception into the Church. This day—the day on which our dear Lord first visits you in the Sacrament of His Love, will be a truly blissful day for you. One of the most beautiful letters I have ever received came from a convert—a former Grand Master of the Freemasons—who wrote to me immediately after he had received his first Communion after his admission into the Catholic Church.

A FINAL WORD

Some converts enter the Church with great emotion, while others experience little or no emotion. In fact, some, like Monsignor Robert Hugh Benson (son of the Anglican Archbishop of Canterbury), feel quite dry and without sentiment or feeling as they cross the threshold of the true Church. And even those who were bubbling over with the sweetest emotions as they entered the fold of Peter will realize, as time goes by, the truth of that statement which Cardinal Newman (though not referring to converts) made: "Alas! what are we doing all life long, but unlearning the world's poetry and attaining to its prose?" Feeling or sentiment, my dear convert, is an unreliable guide; reason, and above all faith, must guide us. The just "live by faith." But ever bear in mind that faith is the prelude to the everlasting vision of God, in which our final happiness consists.

NEWMAN'S FERVID APPEAL

When his deep reading, his careful reasoning, and his earnest prayer had at long last led John Henry Newman "o'er moor and fen, o'er crag and torrent, till the night was gone," and he was about to take the irrevocable step, he wrote the following sublime appeal as a suitable conclusion to a yet unfinished work:

"Such were the thoughts concerning the 'Blessed Vision of Peace', of one whose long-continued petition had been that the Most Merciful would not despise the work of His own hands, nor leave him to himself; while yet his eyes were dim, and his breast laden, and he could but employ Reason in the things of Faith. And now, dear reader, time is short, eternity is long. Put not from you what you have here found; regard it not as mere matter of present controversy; set not out to refute it, and looking about for the best way of doing so; seduce not yourself with the imagination that it comes of disappointment, or disgust, or restlessness, or wounded feeling, or undue sensibility, or other weakness. Wrap not yourself round in the associations of years past; nor determine that to be truth which you wish to be so, nor make an idol of cherished anticipations. Time is short, eternity is long."